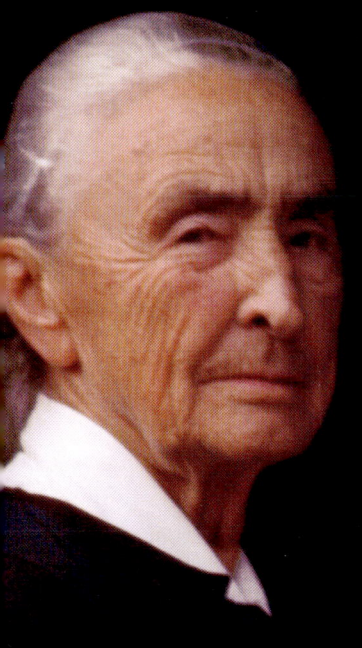
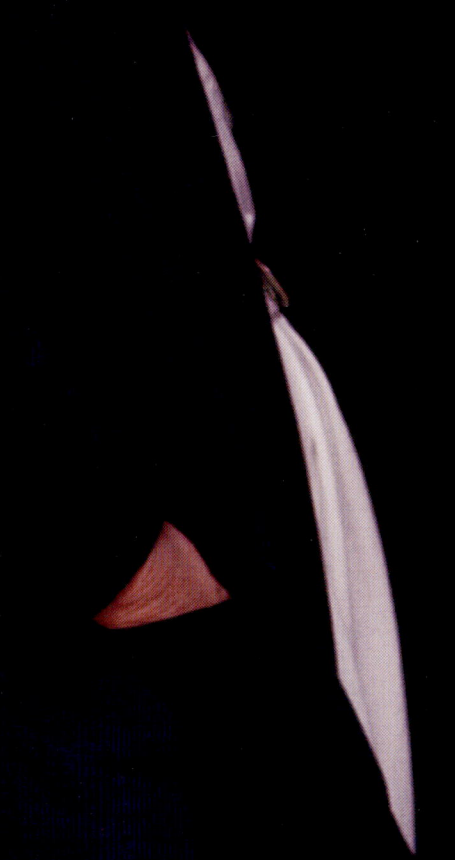

Georgia O'Keeffe

Georgia O'Keeffe
A LIFE WELL LIVED

Malcolm Varon

Foreword by Cody Hartley

Introduction by Barbara Buhler Lynes

University of New Mexico Press | Albuquerque

I dedicate this book to all of you who draw inspiration from Georgia O'Keeffe's life and work and from whose example you have garnered the courage to lead a life of authenticity and self-fulfillment regardless of the obstacles you have encountered along the way.

Contents

Foreword

Photography was always important to Georgia O'Keeffe. As a young artist she was fascinated by the way photographers were beginning to see the world in radical new ways. In her own effort to say something boldly original in her artwork, she drew on photography's capacity for minimalism. The work of Paul Strand, and his ability to focus tightly on his subject—getting so close that details turned into abstract compositions—had a significant influence on O'Keeffe, as did the work of other modernists who used the technical constraints of the camera as a creative and expressive challenge.

Equally many photographers pursued O'Keeffe as a subject. They were as much fascinated by her presence and personality as by her artwork. Her distinctive appearance appealed to artists from her earliest days as a student, when classmates would ask her to model. Despite her choice to pursue a life in art rather than a life as an artist's model, she became the great subject of Alfred Stieglitz, appearing in hundreds of his photographs. In time she became one of the most photographed women of the twentieth century. Yet of all the photographers who portrayed O'Keeffe, only two were entrusted by her to photograph her actual artwork: Stieglitz and Malcolm Varon.

Readers who have discovered O'Keeffe through reproductions of her artwork have Varon to thank more than anyone. From her own lavishly illustrated autobiography, published by Viking Press in 1976, and the exhaustive *Georgia O'Keeffe: Catalogue Raisonné* compiled by scholar Barbara Buhler Lynes and published in 1999 by the National Gallery of Art and the Georgia O'Keeffe Foundation, to many exhibition catalogues and art publications, Varon's photographs of O'Keeffe's artwork maintain the highest standard, established by O'Keeffe herself, for quality by accurately capturing her refined surfaces and color. To this day his photographs continue to be a primary source for many exhibition catalogues and reproductions, a further testament to the enduring quality of his talent and skill as a photographer. Thousands of transparencies produced by Varon are maintained as part of the Georgia O'Keeffe Museum's archive, providing an unparalleled record of her work.

As Varon relates, he was auditioned and his work was approved by Doris Bry, who served as O'Keeffe's close associate for thirty years, and then by O'Keeffe herself. Perhaps there is no higher compliment to his talent than to have his work pass the careful scrutiny of the artist herself. One can imagine few more discerning judges. To satisfy O'Keeffe—who had known many of the finest photographers of her century and lived with and worked alongside one of the world's first great art photographers—was no easy feat.

With his characteristic humility, Varon describes his experience staying at Abiquiú and photographing artwork for several landmark publications. Through his lens he recorded O'Keeffe's artwork and, in time, was invited to also capture some of her life in Abiquiú. The results are some of the finest, most insightful images from the last decades of her life. In his photographs we get an inside glimpse, as if we had the privilege of visiting the artist ourselves. His color images in particular bring a renewed sense of her vibrancy. To see O'Keeffe, who was often photographed in black and white and was so often dressed in black and white, in full, vibrant color makes her more accessible to us as a person, as an individual rather than a distant icon. His written account is filled with admiration and respect, conveying a sincerity that must certainly have been appreciated by an artist who had achieved public renown and sought to maintain her privacy as fans seeking an audience boldly ignored gates and private-property signs.

Varon's account of those visits offers wonderful insights into O'Keeffe's personality and the network of friends and caretakers that surrounded her, and it illustrates the day-to-day life at her New Mexican homes. His sensitivity helps us understand her eternally vivid personality, her keen intelligence, and her too-often overlooked kindness and sensitivity. We are fortunate that Varon has documented O'Keeffe's artwork to share with the world and, moreover, that he has recorded her likeness and personality in his images and words.

CODY HARTLEY
DIRECTOR, GEORGIA O'KEEFFE MUSEUM

Acknowledgments

I would like to thank Elise McHugh for her skill and expertise in editing my text, the choice of images to be included in my book, and her patient and expert shepherding of me through the production hoops every step of the way from the initial idea stage through to the book's final publication.

I greatly thank and want to express my appreciation for the staff at UNM Press for their dedication, enthusiasm, and professionalism, and for their unwavering guidance in the process of bringing this book to publication.

I would especially like to thank Cody Hartley, Barbara Buhler Lynes, and Stuart Ashman for their important role in initially expressing to UNM Press their positive reaction to the idea of this book and their expression of encouragement to UNM Press to go forward with the process of publication. In addition I want to express my great appreciation to Cody Hartley and Barbara Buhler Lynes for agreeing to write the forward and introductory essays in the book.

To Cody Hartley as director of the Georgia O'Keeffe Museum, the museum itself, and the museum staff, I want to express my incalculable gratitude for their generous financial support for the book project and for the time and effort they contributed to the publication of this book.

Finally I particularly want to thank and express my great indebtedness and gratitude to my longtime friend and colleague Cathy Carver for her invaluable material and emotional support and her encouragement to persevere during the long and arduous process of presenting this book as an idea and seeing it through to its final fruition.

Introduction

BARBARA BUHLER LYNES

The photographs in this volume are remarkable. On the one hand, they uncannily refer to many photographs made of Georgia O'Keeffe by some of America's best-known photographers, in part because of similarities of formal pose (head in profile or three-quarter view) and surroundings (such as O'Keeffe's portal at her Ghost Ranch house): Ansel Adams, Philippe Halsman, John Leongard, Yousuf Karsh, Irving Penn, Alfred Stieglitz, Andy Warhol, and Todd Webb, to name only a few.[1] On the other hand, they offer a newly direct, unfiltered portrait of the artist at ninety, the people she saw on a daily basis, her houses in Abiquiú and Ghost Ranch, and the stunning landscape surrounding them in 1977.[2]

O'Keeffe is keenly aware of herself and the image she projects in most of Varon's photographs, having crafted how she wanted to be known for decades. She presents herself as a serious, independent, intelligent, determined, and self-realized artist (pages 15, 17, 18, 19, 21, 28, and 31). Her idea of herself had gained tremendous momentum seven years before Varon photographed her as a result of her retrospective exhibition at the Whitney Museum of American Art in 1970.

It catapulted her into the limelight as well as into the hearts and minds of the thousands who saw it or read its catalogue, especially feminists, who then adopted O'Keeffe as their heroine (despite her subsequent lack of cooperation with them).[3] Such attention paralleled what O'Keeffe had experienced in 1916, at the age of twenty-nine, when Stieglitz, a leading voice in the New York art community, brought the then-unknown O'Keeffe into the spotlight with an exhibition he organized that included her work at his famous avant-garde gallery, 291.[4]

Before Varon photographed O'Keeffe, she had completed a book about herself that offered a great deal of new information about who and what she was,

Georgia O'Keeffe.[5] It was published in 1976 and sold out immediately. It further solidified her place in the psyche of the art community and general public, and it helped O'Keeffe define her concept of herself. Varon's photographs further personify the latter as they shed new light on the artist.[6]

For example, Varon is the first professional photographer to capture O'Keeffe at close range since Stieglitz photographed her in the 1910s and 1920s. Varon catches her as she is about to burst out laughing (page 26) and then as she laughs unabashedly (page 27) in response to something said, obviously feeling very much at ease with Varon. Adams had photographed her nearly smiling in 1937 in a now-famous image of her glancing slyly at Orville Cox, a ranch hand from Ghost Ranch who had accompanied O'Keeffe, Adams, and others on a trip through the Southwest that year.[7]

O'Keeffe smiled in many snapshots made by friends known and unknown, such as those of her in Canyon, Texas, in the 1910s and photographs taken by Rebecca Strand in 1929 and by Maria Chabot in the 1940s.[8] Yet O'Keeffe rarely smiled in any of the thousands of professional photographs made since the mid-1920s. At ninety, she knew that revealing a then relatively unknown, engagingly human side of her personality—her keen, often biting sense of humor—would not compromise her image, which she had successfully crafted for decades and which she projects in many of Varon's photographs and through which she continues to be known. This image differs vastly from the sexualized image of her Stieglitz had created at the beginning of her career and through which he promoted her and her art in annual exhibitions until his death in 1946.[9]

O'Keeffe did not openly reject Stieglitz's Freudian ideas about her art until much later in her career, but she began a silent campaign to counteract them immediately after they dominated the critical reviews of her retrospective exhibition, which Stieglitz organized in 1923. She subsequently shifted the emphasis in her art away from pure abstraction and toward recognizable forms in images dating from the mid-1920s, for which she remains best known—her large-scale flower paintings. She would return to abstraction late in her career, when she worked with it almost exclusively from the 1970s until she stopped making art in the mid-1980s.[10]

She also presented herself to the media and public as she felt she was and as she wished to be known: a serious, uncompromising, self-determined artist. But after Stieglitz's death in 1946, she openly pursued establishing her own identity through the many photographs made of her by professional photographers, many of which were published in widely read newspapers and popular magazines, including *LIFE*, *Look*, *Newsweek*, the *New Yorker*, *Time*, the *New York Times*, *Town and Country*, *Vanity Fair*, and *Vogue*, among others.[11] By 1977, with age on her side, she had succeeded in replacing Stieglitz's idea of her with her own.[12]

When Varon photographed her looking directly into the camera (pages 15, 17, and 28), she seems to make eye contact with the viewer despite her inability to see except peripherally. Partial blindness, however, did not compromise her confident demeanor—an aspect of her personality that Stieglitz had captured, especially in the photographs he made after her return to New York in 1929. At this time she began to spend the first of many summers painting in northern New Mexico, knowing she had found a place that would provide ongoing nourishment for her art.[13] And, by 1977, she had fully realized her childhood dream of making her way as an artist and had long been recognized as one of America's most important modernists and icons. Varon's photographs convey her realization of this success and the knowledge age brings, components of O'Keeffe's demeanor that were beginning to emerge in the 1960s in the work of other professional photographers mentioned previously.

Her self-image is stark and severe when she poses in profile for Varon (pages 19 and 29), images that recall the stunning profile photographs Stieglitz made of her in 1923, 1927, and 1929, for example, as well as the now-famous photographs of her in profile by Halsman (1948), Karsh (1956), Tony Vaccaro (1960), Eliot Porter (1961), and Arnold Newman (1968). These photographs captured the imagination of the American public in that O'Keeffe was seen as a loner and pioneer who had left New York, then rose to the center of the American art community while living and working in seeming isolation amid the dry harshness of the northern New Mexico desert—a landscape whose uncompromising nature paralleled her own.[14]

Yet only Varon's profile portrait of her (page 19) juxtaposes a close-up view of her face with nature—her beloved Pedernal, the mountain she saw from the patio of her Ghost Ranch house and painted frequently, which is now a hallmark of her work. Varon establishes a visual link between O'Keeffe and the world of nature with which she was profoundly engaged, whose energies, vitality, and sexual and provocative forms were actualized in her paintings, especially her large-scale images of flowers seen as if from close up, which have prompted frequent Freudian readings of them. Some continue to view them as a revelation of female sexuality despite their universality in representing the pulsing life forces that animate all living forms.

3

Varon's photographs are the first extensive series of color photographs of and about O'Keeffe. We see the aging artist from up close, white and grey hair sometimes held in place by a transparent white net, with a single hair occasionally escaping such confinement (pages 17, 28, and 29). Time has deeply wrinkled and age-spotted her skin, her eyebrows are half gone, and there is a fuzz of black hair on her upper lip. Had she known how closely Varon photographed her, she might have put a stop to it. Or, perhaps, she knew exactly what he was doing.

Varon also photographed O'Keeffe standing in profile amid the landscape of colorful cliffs in her backyard at Ghost Ranch, which she had often painted (page 16). These images again are the first to depict her there, although Leongard had photographed her walking in the front yard of her Ghost Ranch house toward the Pedernal in 1966, and Vaccaro (1960) and Newman (1968) had used the landscape behind Ghost Ranch as a backdrop when photographing her with an easel that either supported an unpainted canvas (Newman) or displayed her famous bone painting, *Pelvis Series, Red with Yellow*, 1945 (Vacarro).

4

In these Varon and Vacarro photographs and in another by Newman, O'Keeffe is in full regalia, wearing the components of a wardrobe she selected that established her signature style: a wide-brimmed black hat, a black wrap dress, a Hector Aguilar silver-and-black leather belt, the silver pin of her initials made for and given to her by artist Alexander Calder (barely visible on her dress on page 16), and soft shoes. She had been developing aspects of this severe, minimalist style since the mid-1920s by dressing nearly exclusively in black and white.

She was first photographed in her broad-brimmed, black hat by Adams (1937), and she wears it in photographs by Halsman (1948), Vaccaro (1960), Webb (1963), and Bruce Weber (1984), who was the last professional to photograph her. She first wore the wrap dress when posing for Vacarro in 1960 and then for Webb and Leongard later in that decade.[15] She wears the Calder pin in a 1942 photograph by John Candelario as well as when she posed for Carl Van Vechten in 1950 and for many others who photographed her in the 1960s and 1970s.

In some Varon photographs, O'Keeffe carries a walking stick (pages 16, 20, 21, 23, and 30), similar to what she was holding in photographs by Stieglitz in the 1920s. She made a point of telling Varon that she did not carry it to steady herself, but rather to ward off rattlesnakes she might encounter on her daily walks through the Ghost Ranch landscape. She was obviously unafraid of such encounters, active, and in relatively good physical shape, although she was frail, vulnerable, and dependent, qualities Varon also captured poignantly several times (pages 30, 38, and 45).

Varon's photographs provide new insight on O'Keeffe's friendship with artist and potter Juan Hamilton, which began in 1972 when he was twenty-six and she was eighty-five. Their relationship prompted speculation about whether or not they were lovers, which amused and delighted O'Keeffe (they were not).[16] By 1977 Hamilton had become her assistant and had taught her to work in clay after partial blindness stopped her from painting in oil, which kept her active creatively until several years before her death in 1986.[17] Varon photographed them walking, talking, and laughing together (pages 39, 40, and 44), revealing the depth of O'Keeffe's trust in Hamilton and her dependence on him, which can be seen, for example, when she gently and tenderly touches him while looking up and directly into his face (page 38).

The same sense of closeness characterizes them in photographs Varon made of the two on the portal of O'Keeffe's Ghost Ranch house (pages 41 and 42–43). They sit adjacent to the stark, bleached bones O'Keeffe kept on the wall and shelf of the portal, objects she often made the subjects of her work. Varon's photographs of O'Keeffe by herself in the portal with these forms (pages 22 and 24) call to mind those Webb made of her there in the 1960s.

Varon also photographed O'Keeffe either alone or with Hamilton at the Abiquiú house, standing at the door of its dining room (page 36) or within its open patio door, which led into a large room O'Keeffe called the *salita* (pages 18, 35, and 37). The door had fascinated O'Keeffe from the moment she first saw the house in the 1940s, when it was a ruin, and she frequently said that she bought the house because of that door, which she often made the subject of her work.[18]

The image she projects in these photographs at the Abiquiú house seems softer because she is not dressed in her signature regalia but rather in a long, flowing white dress, which she covers partially with a green and black Marimekko coat most probably purchased for her by her former assistant, Doris Bry.[19] The black door and its open, empty dark space frame O'Keeffe and Hamilton, again completely at ease with one another, whether standing side by side or at a distance from one another (pages 35 and 37).

In one Varon photograph Hamilton stands behind and above O'Keeffe, looking directly at the camera with O'Keeffe's head in profile and slightly out of focus (page 45). This positioning recalls photographs of O'Keeffe and Stieglitz by Newman (1944) and Cecil Beaton (1946) in which Stieglitz or O'Keeffe are seen either side by side or with one in a position of dominance. Here the youthful Hamilton looms above the aging O'Keeffe, conveying the degree to which he would increasingly oversee, manage, and orchestrate the last nine years of her life.

Another photograph captures the strong, handsome, long-haired Hamilton alone at the back entrance gate of the Abiquiú property (page 46), seemingly aware of the enormous responsibility he has assumed as the assistant, manager, and close friend of one of America's icons. That he resembled Stieglitz as a young man must have stirred O'Keeffe's memories of her life with Stieglitz. Indeed, she would become as dependent on Hamilton at the end of her life as she had been on Stieglitz at the beginning of her career. Had her path not crossed Stieglitz's, we might not know her or her art, and had Hamilton not entered her life, she might not have lived as long as she did.

Among the many photographs Varon made of O'Keeffe's Abiquiú house, only three depict interiors: the roofless room, the kitchen, and an adobe fireplace ablaze with light, one of many in the house (pages 54, 69, and 58). Earlier photographers who made the house the subject of their work focused on its interior spaces, such as the color photographs Ralph Looney made in 1962 and those of Balthazar Korab in 1965. Varon's images convey the character of the house's exterior—its adobe-colored walls and their inconsistencies of surface, color, and texture and how they are sometimes streaked or marked by water stains or supporting hand-hewn ladders (pages 52, 56, 74, 78, 79, and 82).

Varon photographed the entrance to her Abiquiú studio, with an overgrown Tamarisk tree in full bloom on the left (page 80–81), rather than the interior of this space, which had been the subject of photographs by Laura Gilpin, Korab, and Vacarro. Varon photographs the formal entrance of the house, where Halsman, Karsh, Vacarro, and Newman had photographed her. Her absence from the entrance of the house, well known by her presence in it in earlier photographs, foreshadows the permanence of her absence from it after her death. He also photographed O'Keeffe's beloved patio and door (pages 59 and 75) and paths outside the house leading to or from O'Keeffe's garden, where she famously grew a great deal of her own food (pages 55, 78, and 79).

Varon was the first to photograph people who worked for O'Keeffe (pages 67 and 68) as well as her sister Claudia, who often helped with the garden (page 70). In doing so he allows us to imagine her daily interactions with them as well as with one of her many beloved Chow dogs (page 66). Varon also made the stunningly colorful but harsh and rugged landscape surrounding O'Keeffe's Abiquiú and Ghost Ranch houses, as well as areas adjacent to both, the subject of his work.

Had Mary Lynn Kotz not interviewed O'Keeffe while Varon was working for O'Keeffe in Abiquiú in July of 1977, he probably would never have photographed her. But he had the good fortune of being in the right place at the right time, having already proven himself as a professional photographer to the artist, as he had photographed her art and, in reviewing and approving each for inclusion in *Georgia O'Keeffe*, she felt that he had captured their essence, despite her limited vision.[20] His photographs are the first to actualize the contradictions that were complicating O'Keeffe's life: she is old but active and vital, confident and self-assured but frail and vulnerable, independent but dependent. At the same time, she radiates the wisdom of age and a life well lived, awareness of her spectacular success, and, despite her ninety years, an alluring and provocative androgyny, the latter of which had fascinated Stieglitz in the 1910s and upon which he in part capitalized to promote his sexualized ideas about her and her art.

Moreover, Varon's photographs speak to O'Keeffe's mastery of knowing how to pose for professional photographers, having first learned decades earlier from Stieglitz. But these formal portraits also depict O'Keeffe in candid moments usually present only in snapshots, thus synthesizing candor and formality, qualities apparent only in Stieglitz's photographs of her at Lake George, where they summered at his family's compound, and some Vacarro and Webb photographs of the 1960s. Varon's work thus sheds new light on who O'Keeffe was and how she perceived herself at ninety, providing the most comprehensive view of the artist and her daily life since those Stieglitz made at Lake George from the 1910s until he quit making photographs in the late 1930s.

Notes

1. Varon photographed O'Keeffe in July 1977. For a list of professional photographers of O'Keeffe, see Wanda M. Corn, *Living Modern*, exhibition catalogue, Brooklyn Museum (New York: Prestel, 2017), 199–301. Varon's photographs are dated December 1977 on the list, which is the month some of them were published in Mary Lynn Kotz, "O'Keeffe at 90: Filling a Space in a Beautiful Way, That's What Art Means to Me," *Art News* 77 (December 1977): 36–45.

2. Ghost Ranch is eighteen miles north of the village of Abiquiú. It was owned by Arthur Pack, who operated it as a dude ranch. In 1933 he built a house there for his family, which O'Keefe purchased from him in 1940: Ranchos de los Burros, some two miles from the ranch's main headquarters. O'Keeffe purchased the Abiquiú house in 1945.

3. See Lloyd Goodrich and Doris Bry, *Georgia O'Keeffe*, exhibition catalogue, Whitney Museum of American Art (New York: Praeger, 1970); Judy Chicago and Miriam Schapiro, "Female Imagery," *Womanspace Journal* 1 (Summer 1973): 11, 13; Linda Nochlin, "The Twentieth Century: Issues, Problems, Controversies," in Ann Sutherland Harris and Linda Nochlin, *Women Artists: 1550–1950* (New York: Alfred A. Knopf, 1977), 59n209. O'Keeffe also would not allow Lawrence Alloway to reproduce six of her paintings in a late-decade article that examined, among other things, Chicago's and Schapiro's interpretations of her work. See Lawrence Alloway, "Author's Note," in "Notes on Georgia O'Keeffe's Imagery," *Womanart* 1 (Spring–Summer 1977), 18; and Irene Moss, "Georgia O'Keeffe and 'these people,'" *Feminist Art Journal* 2 (Spring 1973): 14. For an assessment of O'Keeffe's response to such interpretations of her art, see Barbara Buhler Lynes, "O'Keeffe and Feminism: A Problem of Position," in *The Expanding Discourse: Feminism and Art History*, ed. Norma Broude and Mary D. Garrard (New York: HarperCollins, 1992), 436–49. For an analysis of feminism in twentieth-century America and O'Keeffe's place within it, see Linda M. Grasso, *Equal Under the Sky: Georgia O'Keeffe and Twentieth-Century Feminism* (Albuquerque: University of New Mexico Press, 2017).

4. For an assessment of the critical reception of O'Keeffe's art, see Barbara Buhler Lynes, *O'Keeffe, Stieglitz, and the Critics, 1916–1929* (Ann Arbor, MI: UMI Research Press, 1989, and Chicago: University of Chicago Press, 1991); and "Georgia O'Keeffe, An American Phenomenon: Issues of Identity," in *Georgia O'Keeffe*, exhibition catalogue, ed. Barbara Buhler Lynes (Milan: Skira Editore, 2011), 13–20.

5. See Georgia O'Keeffe, *Georgia O'Keeffe* (New York: Viking Press, 1976).

6. Perry Miller Adato's 1977 groundbreaking film about Georgia O'Keeffe further solidified O'Keeffe's idea of herself and also offered a great deal of new information about the artist. It aired on November 15, 1977. See Perry Miller Adato, producer and director, *Georgia O'Keeffe*, Videotape, 59 minutes, produced by WNET/THIRTEEN for Women in Art, 1977. Portrait of an Artist, no. 1, series distributed by Films, Inc. / Home Vision, New York.

7. From late September though early October, O'Keeffe traveled with Ansel Adams, Orville Cox, and David McAlpin to sites in Colorado and Arizona, including the Grand Canyon and Canyon de Chelly.

8. For information on snapshots of O'Keeffe, see Amy Von Lintel, *Georgia O'Keeffe: Watercolors* (Santa Fe, NM: Radius Books and the Georgia O'Keeffe Museum, 2016). Archives at the Georgia O'Keeffe Museum provide online access to these snapshots.

9. Stieglitz associated all human creativity with sexual energies, and his 1919 unpublished essay, "Woman in Art," asserted that women's creativity emerged from their wombs. See Lynes, *O'Keeffe, Stieglitz, and the Critics*, 33. "Woman in Art" was partially published in Dorothy Norman, *Alfred Stieglitz: An American Seer* (New York: Random House, 1973), 136–38. In a 1921 exhibition of his own art, Steiglitz created a sensation by including sharply focused, "straight" photographs of O'Keeffe's body, a public declaration of the then-scandalous love affair between the thirty-four-year-old, unknown O'Keeffe and the fifty-seven-year-old, married éminence grise of the New York art community. These photographs portrayed her as sensual, naïve, and vulnerable. Whether nude or partially clothed, she is sometimes positioned in front of one of her recently completed, abstract works, a presentation that equates her art with her body and her sexuality. As art critic Henry McBride put it in "O'Keeffe at the Museum," a May 18, 1946, article on O'Keeffe that appeared in the *New York Sun*, "It made a stir. Mona Lisa got but one portrait of herself worth talking about. O'Keeffe got a hundred. It put her at once on the map. Everybody knew the name. She became what is known as a newspaper personality."

10. For an assessment of O'Keeffe's lifelong fascination with abstraction, see Barbara Buhler Lynes, "Georgia O'Keeffe and Abstraction: An Uneasy Peace," in *Georgia O'Keeffe: Abstraction*, exhibition catalogue, Whitney Museum of American Art, the Phillips Collection, Georgia O'Keeffe Museum (New Haven, CT: Yale University Press, 2009), 167–75.

11. In 1939, a decade after O'Keeffe had achieved financial independence, she began to challenge the Freudian interpretations of her work that were first proffered by Stieglitz. She openly disassociated her ideas about her work from theirs in a statement she wrote for the brochure of her exhibition that year: "I made you take time to look at what I saw and when you took time to really notice my flower you hung all your own associations with flowers on my flower and you write about my flower as if I think and see what you think and see of the flower—and I don't." See Barbara Buhler Lynes, *Georgia O'Keeffe: Catalogue Raisonné*, 2 vols. (New Haven and London: Yale University Press in association with the National Gallery of Art [Washington, DC] and the Georgia O'Keeffe Foundation [Santa Fe, NM], 1999), 2: 1099.

12. See Susan Danly, *Georgia O'Keeffe and the Camera: The Art of Identity* (Portland, OR: Portland Museum of Art, 2008); and Lynes, *Georgia O'Keeffe* (2011).

13. O'Keeffe had first visited New Mexico in 1917, and she went there in 1929 as a means of finding new sources of inspiration for her work and finding an alternative to spending summers at the Stieglitz family compound at Lake George, where she was often surrounded by Stieglitz's large family and their many visitors.

14. The perception of O'Keeffe living in isolation is mythic in that the artist was seldom alone while in New Mexico, as she surrounded herself with those who worked for her and often welcomed visiting friends.

15. See Corn, *Living Modern*.

16. See Laurie Lisle, *Portrait of An Artist: A Biography of O'Keeffe* (New York: Washington Square Books, 1980), 410; Roxana Robinson, *Georgia O'Keeffe: A Life* (New York: Harper and Row, 1987), 534; and Hunter Drohojowska-Phelp, *Full Bloom: The Art and Life of Georgia O'Keeffe* (New York: W. W. Norton & Company, Inc., 2004), 520.

17. Hamilton inherited O'Keeffe's estate upon O'Keeffe's death in 1986. Members of the O'Keeffe family sued, and the case was settled out of court, which resulted in, among other things, the formation of the Georgia O'Keeffe Foundation, whose board included Hamilton and members of O'Keeffe's family, among others. When the Foundation dissolved in 2006, it gave O'Keeffe's residual estate to the Georgia O'Keeffe Museum in Santa Fe, New Mexico.

18. "That wall with a door in it was something I had to have. It took me ten years to get it—three more years to fix the house so I could live in it—and after that the wall with a door was painted many times" (O'Keeffe, interview, 1976).

19. O'Keeffe's financial records indicate she paid Bry for dresses.

20. In Perry Miller Adato's 1977 film, *Georgia O'Keeffe*, O'Keeffe is seen reviewing Varon's photographs, indicating that they met her expectations for reproduction in her book. She stated, "It doesn't really matter if the color isn't absolutely right if the picture feels right when you finish the print."

PHOTOGRAPHS

Georgia O'Keeffe

*A Woman of Intense Personality
and Piercing Intelligence*

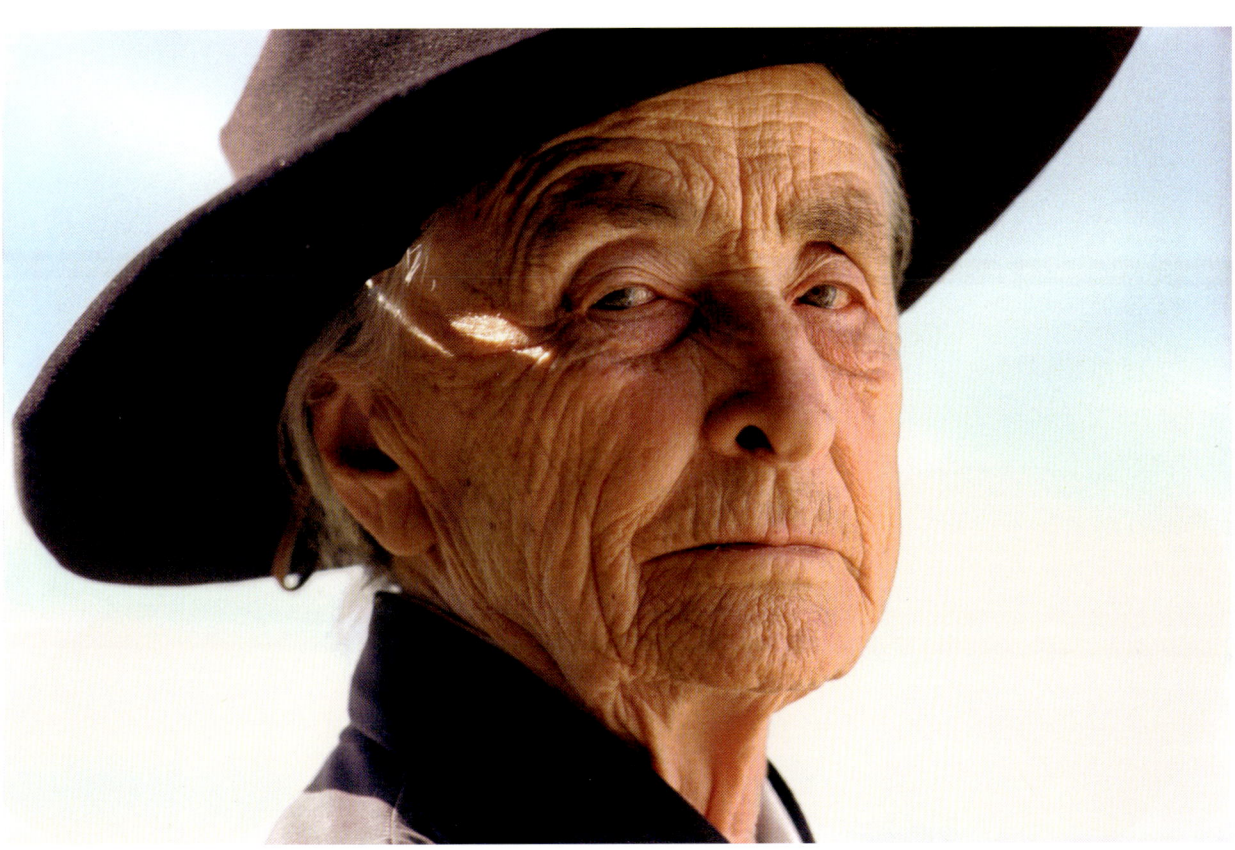

O'Keeffe at Ghost Ranch.

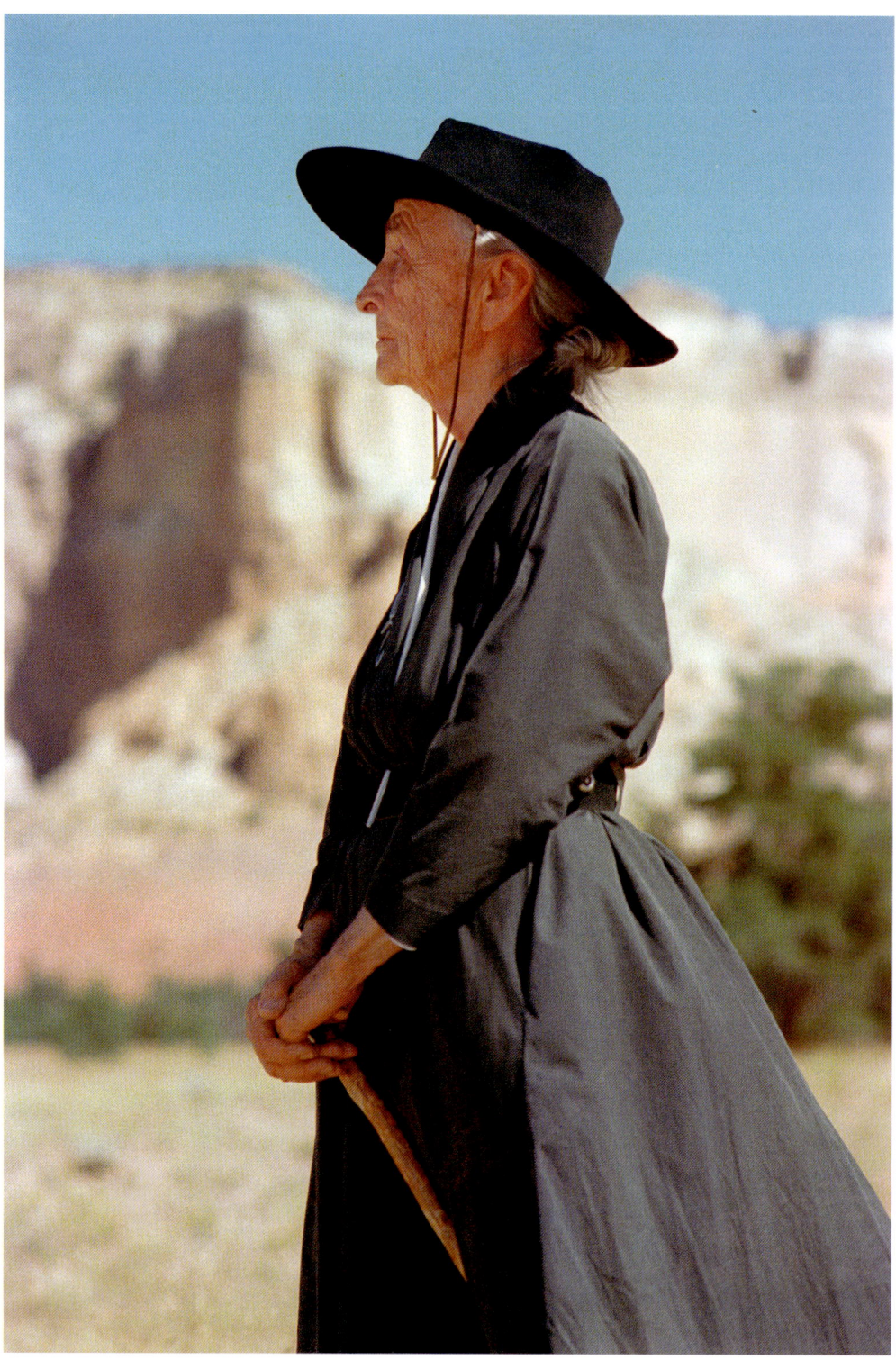

O'Keeffe at Ghost Ranch.

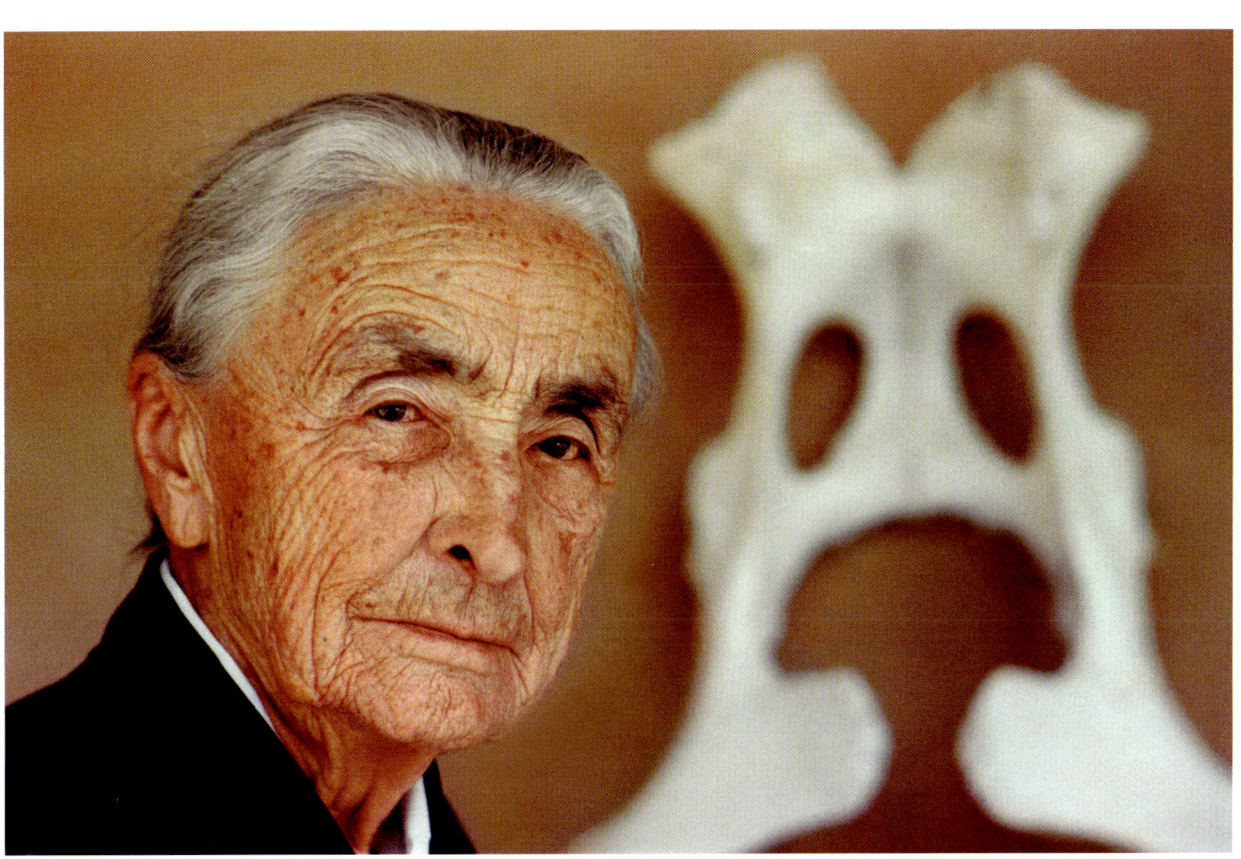

Close-up of O'Keeffe in the patio at Ghost Ranch with
a pelvis bone as a seeming apparition on the wall behind her.

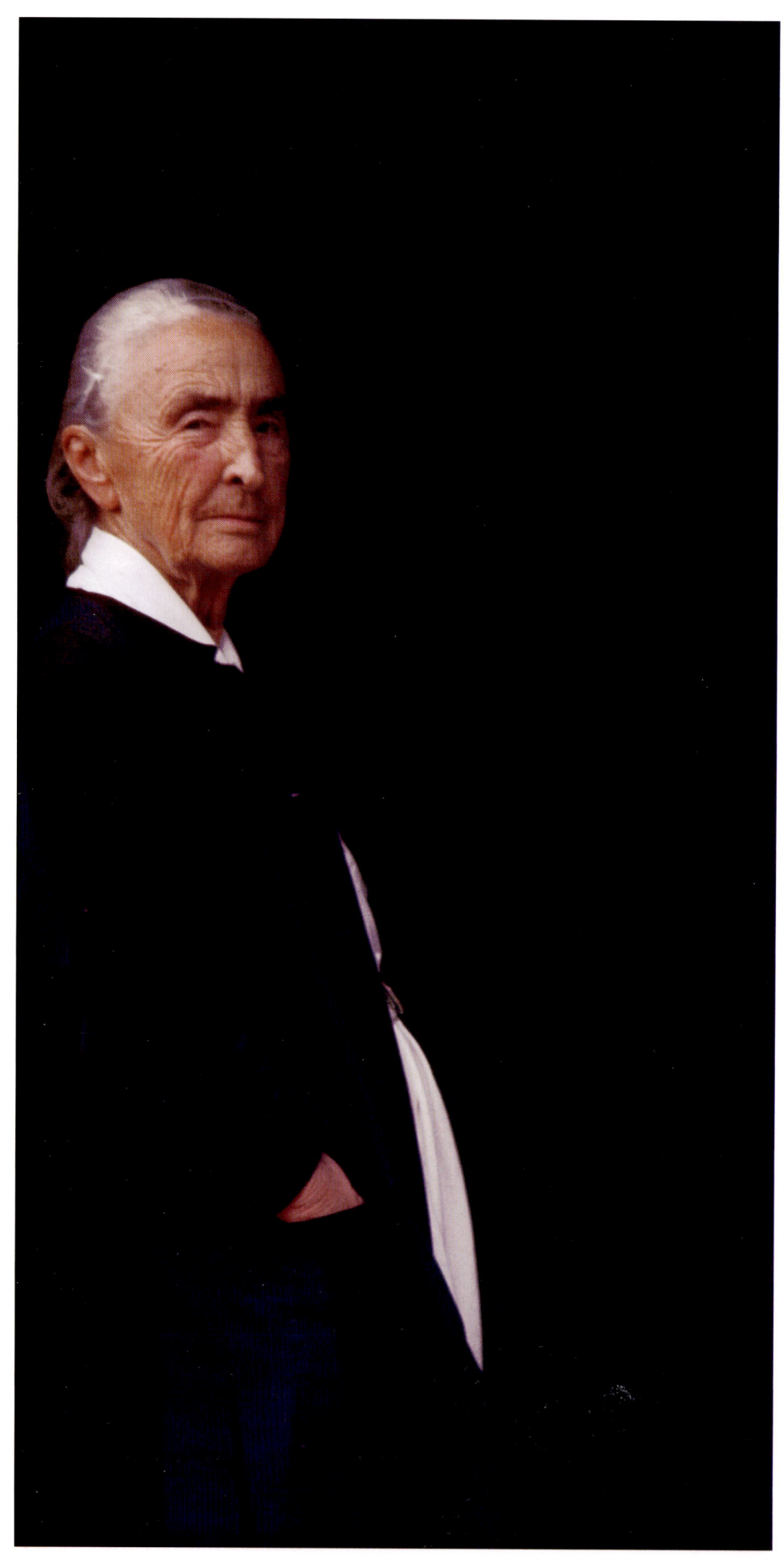

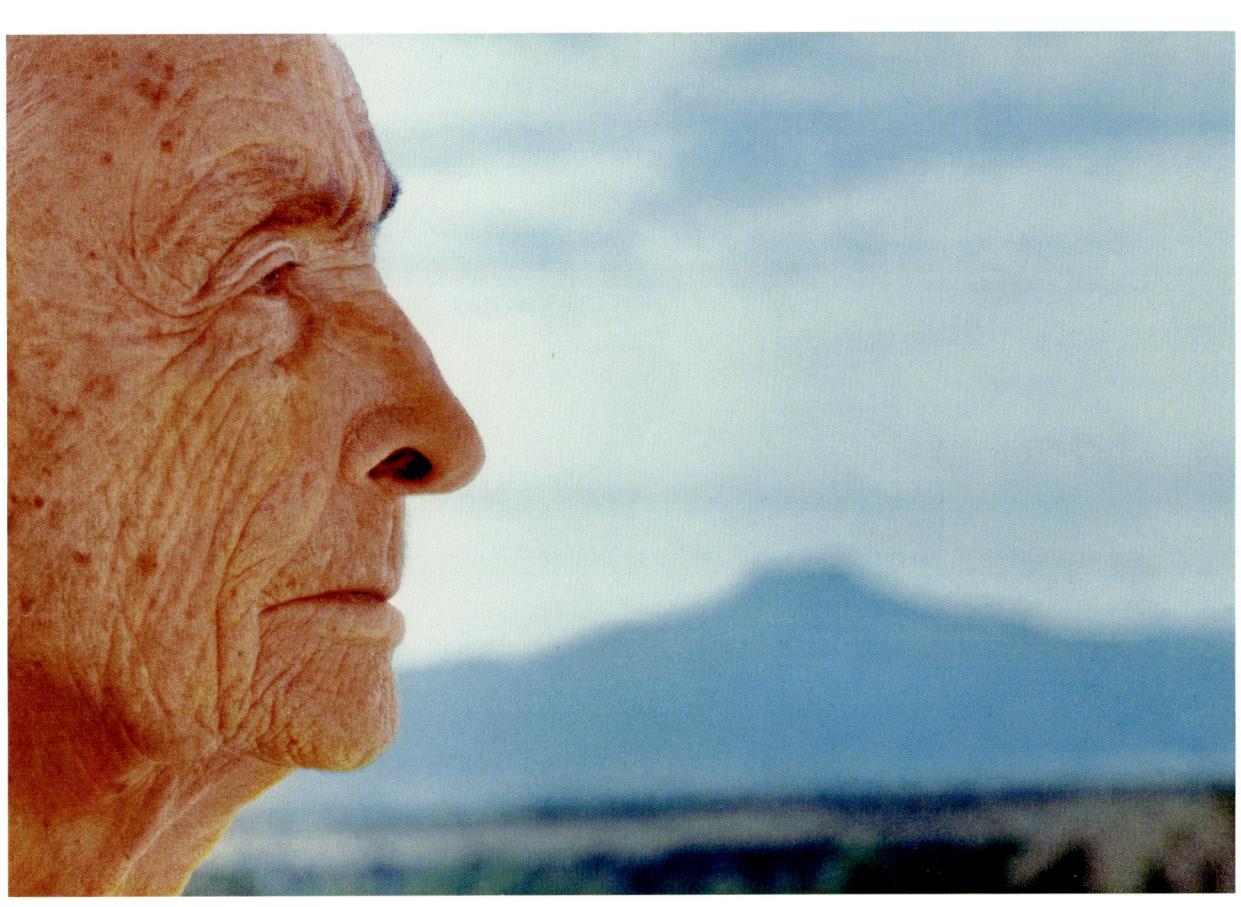

Profile of O'Keeffe at Ghost Ranch. In the background
is the Pedernal, a mountain that is a recurring image in O'Keeffe's paintings.

Opposite page: O'Keeffe in a doorway at Abiquiú.

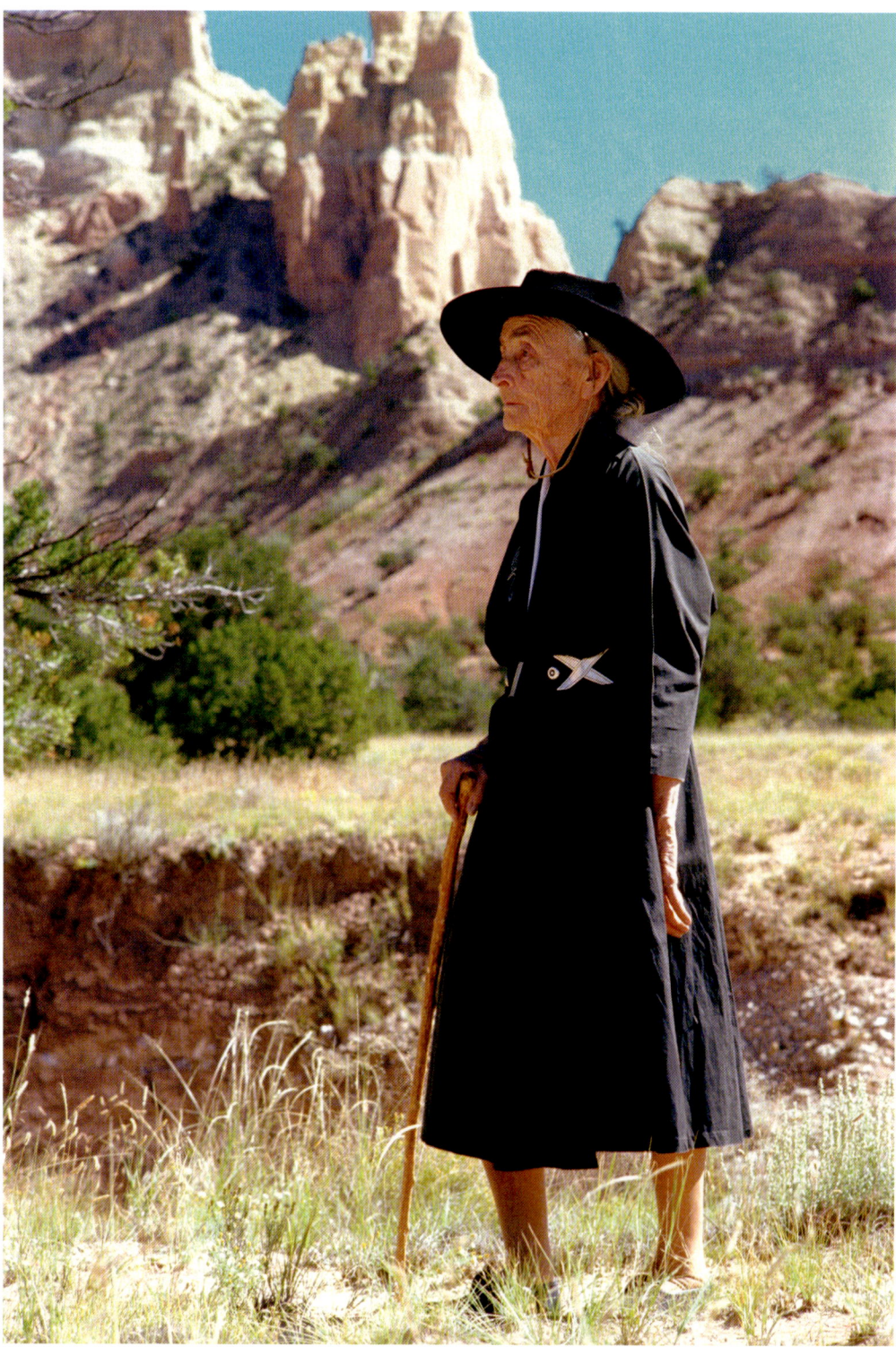

O'Keeffe walking in the field at Ghost Ranch. The cliffs
in the background were the subjects of several O'Keeffe paintings.

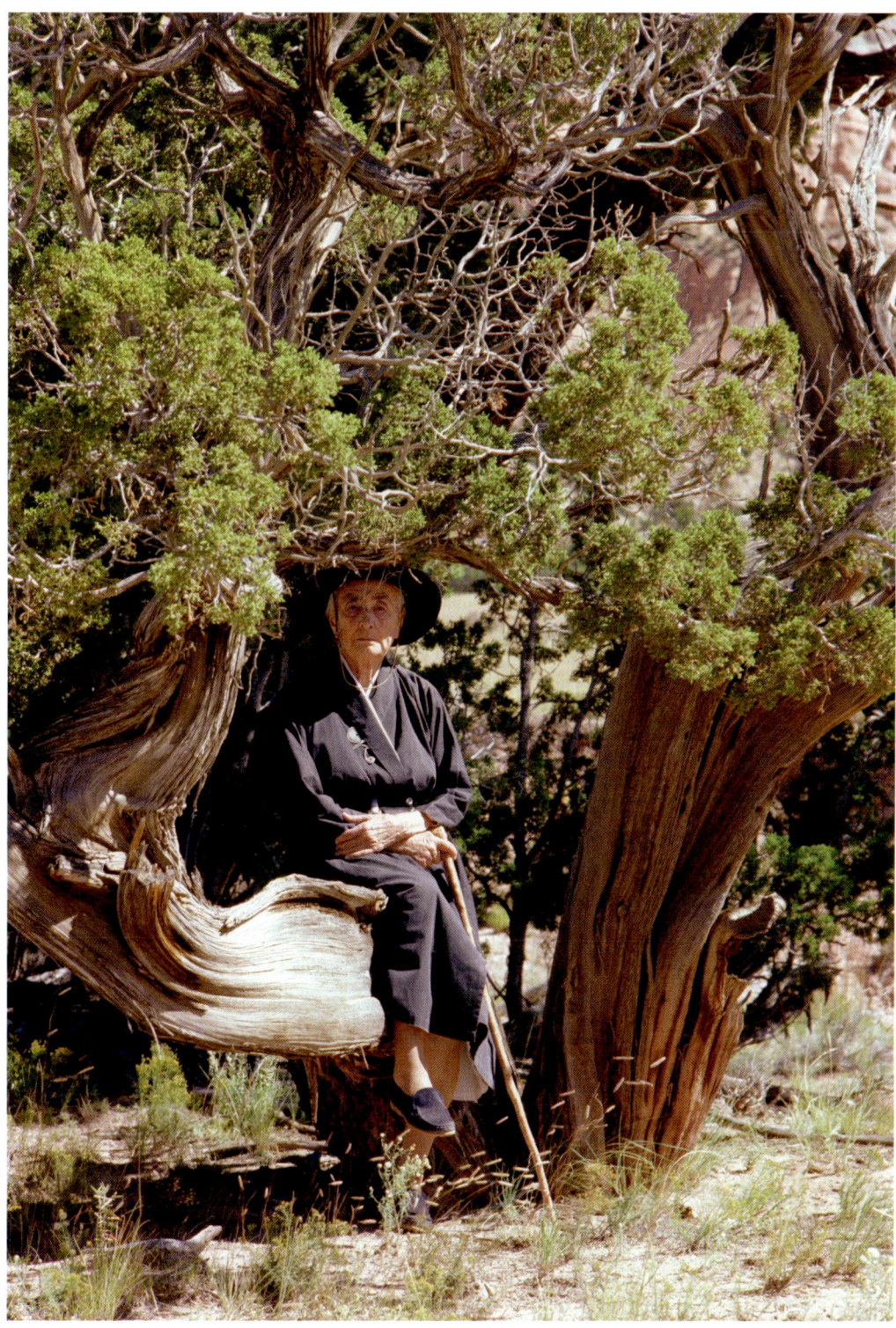

O'Keeffe relaxing on the curved trunk of a tree at Ghost Ranch.

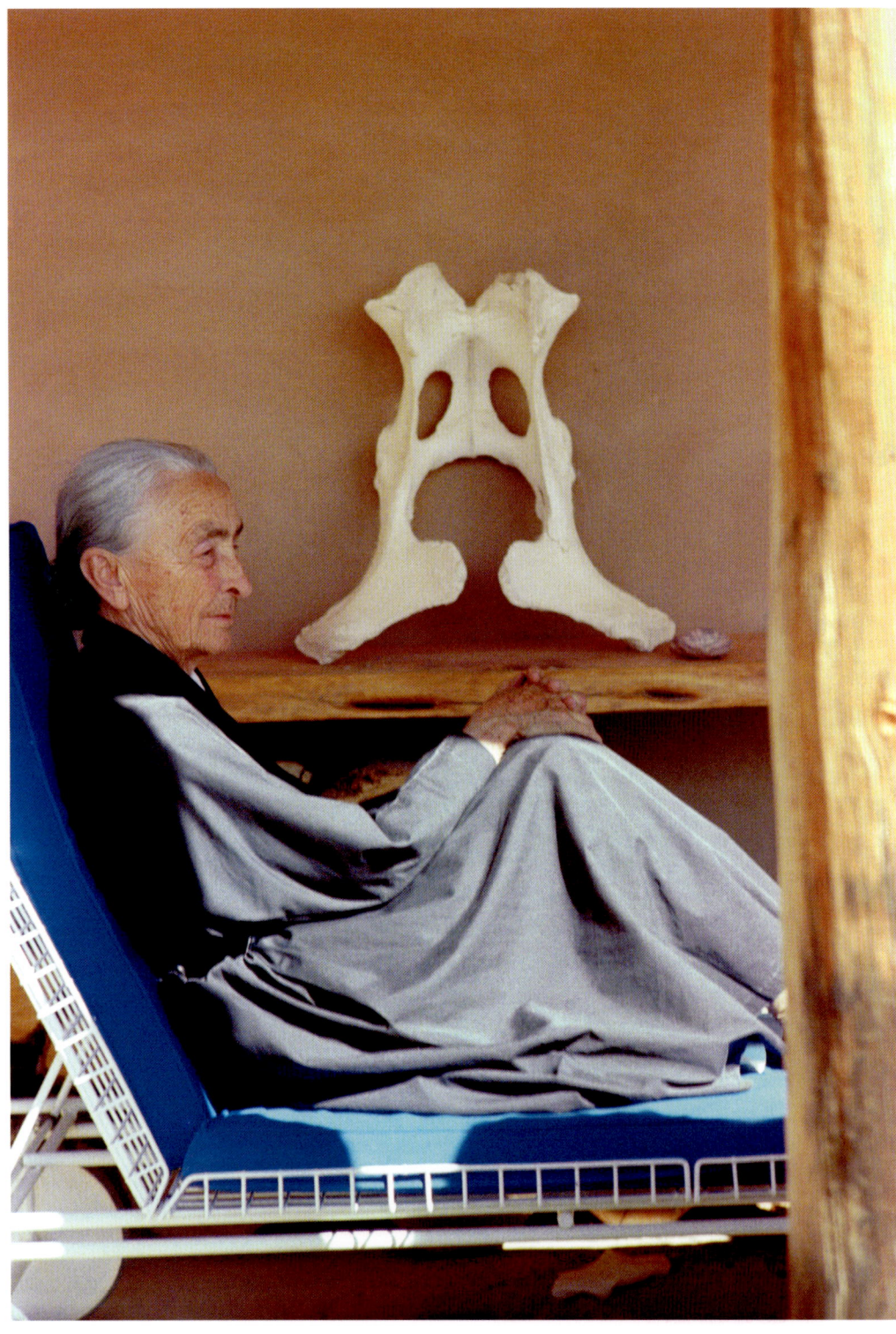

O'Keeffe in the portal of the patio at Ghost Ranch. I took this photo because O'Keeffe sitting in profile with her hand on her knee reminded me of Whistler's *Portrait of the Artist's Mother* (better known as *Whistler's Mother*), the pelvis bone standing in for the picture hanging on the wall in Whistler's painting completing the composition.

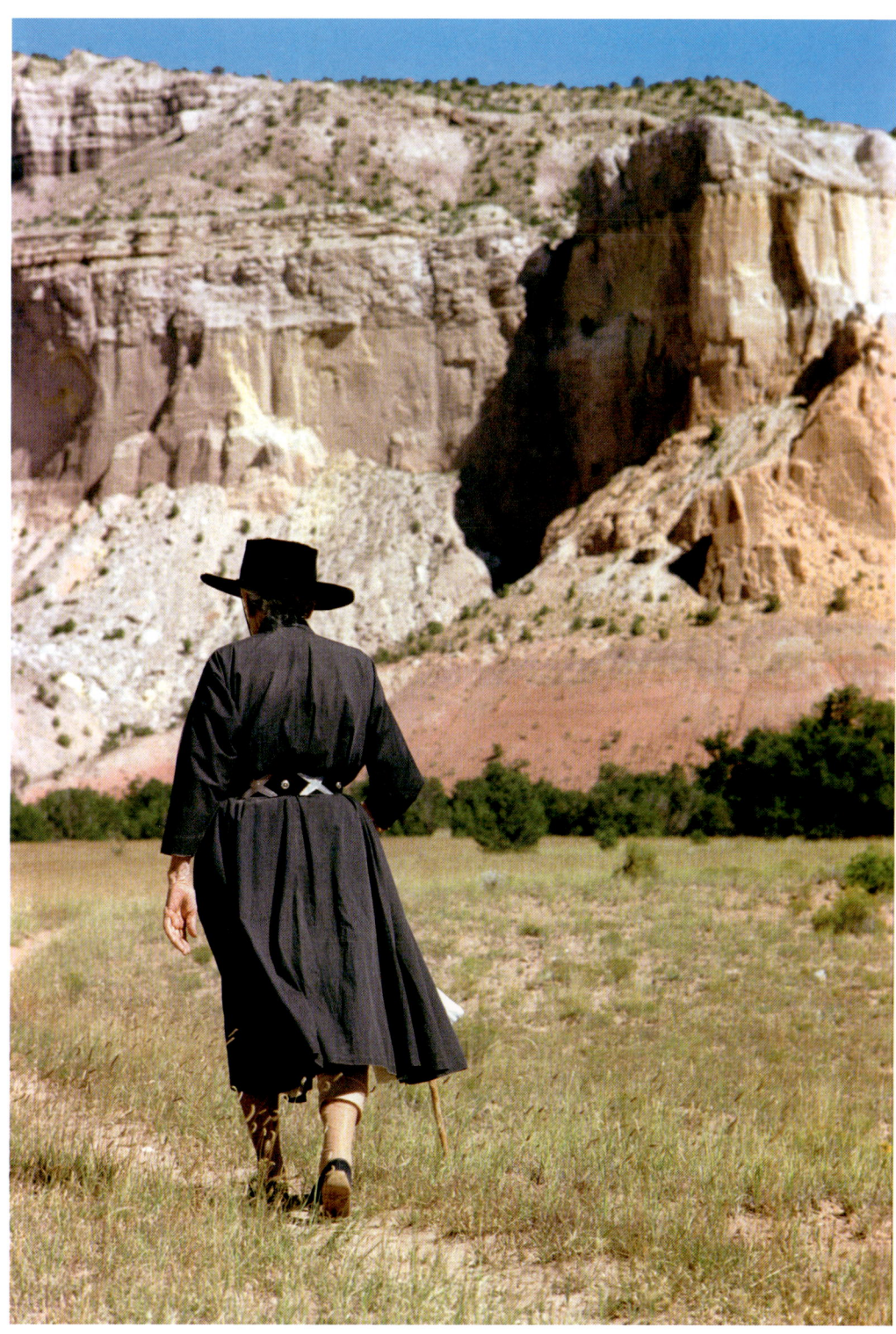

O'Keeffe briskly walking in the field at Ghost Ranch.

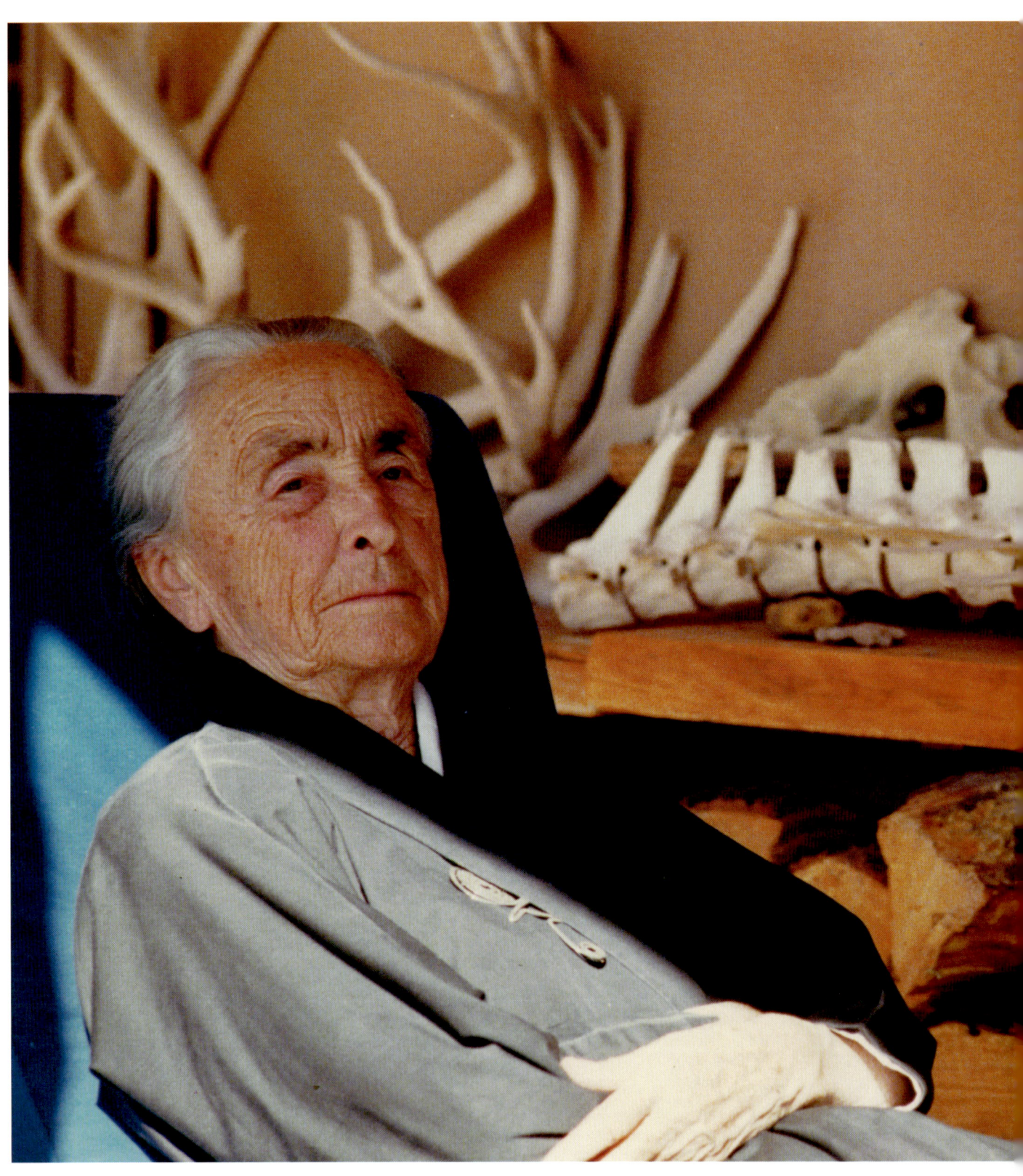

O'Keeffe in the portal of the patio at Ghost Ranch. In the background is one of
the shelves displaying her collection of bones, which were often the subjects of her paintings.

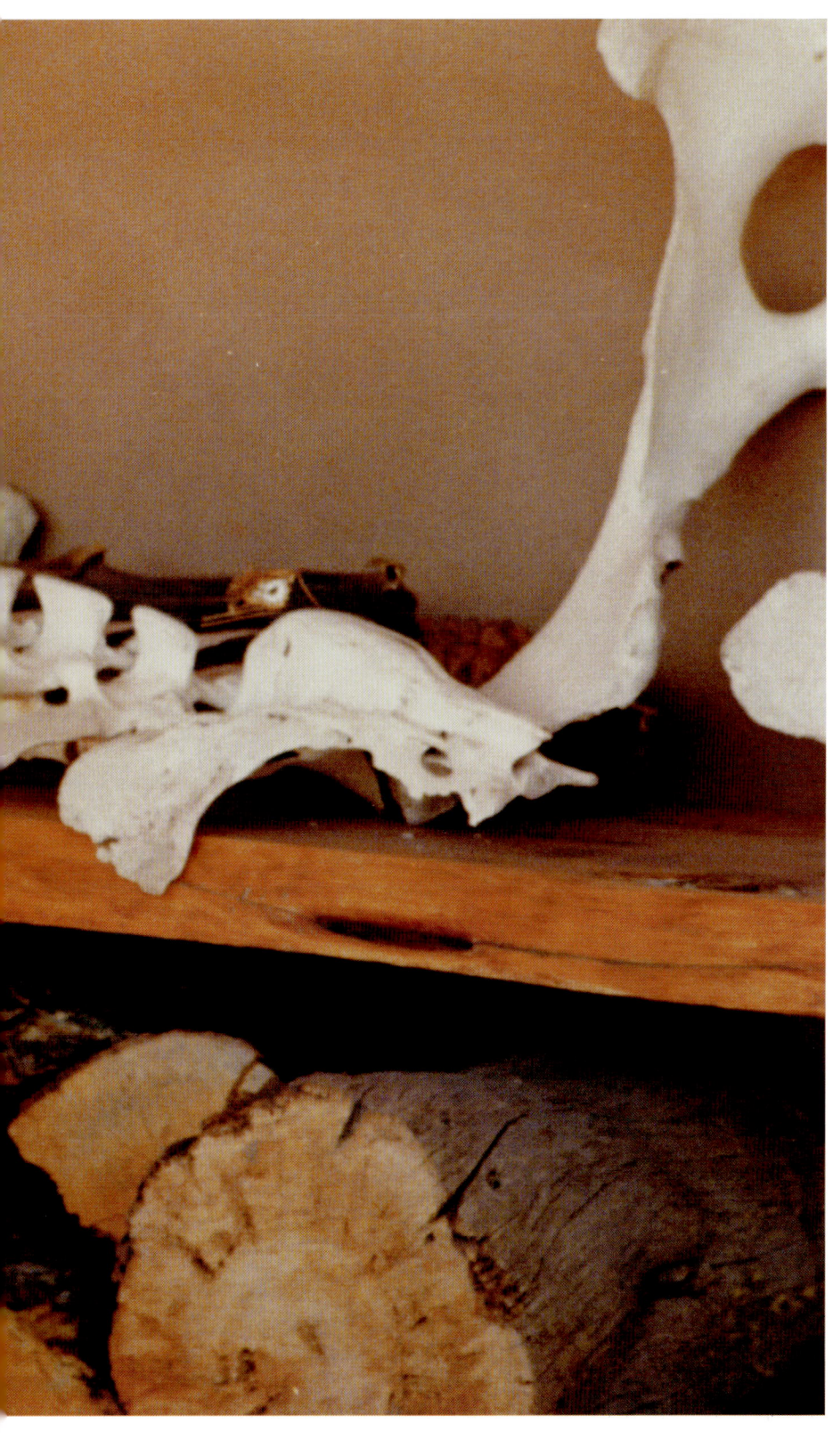

26

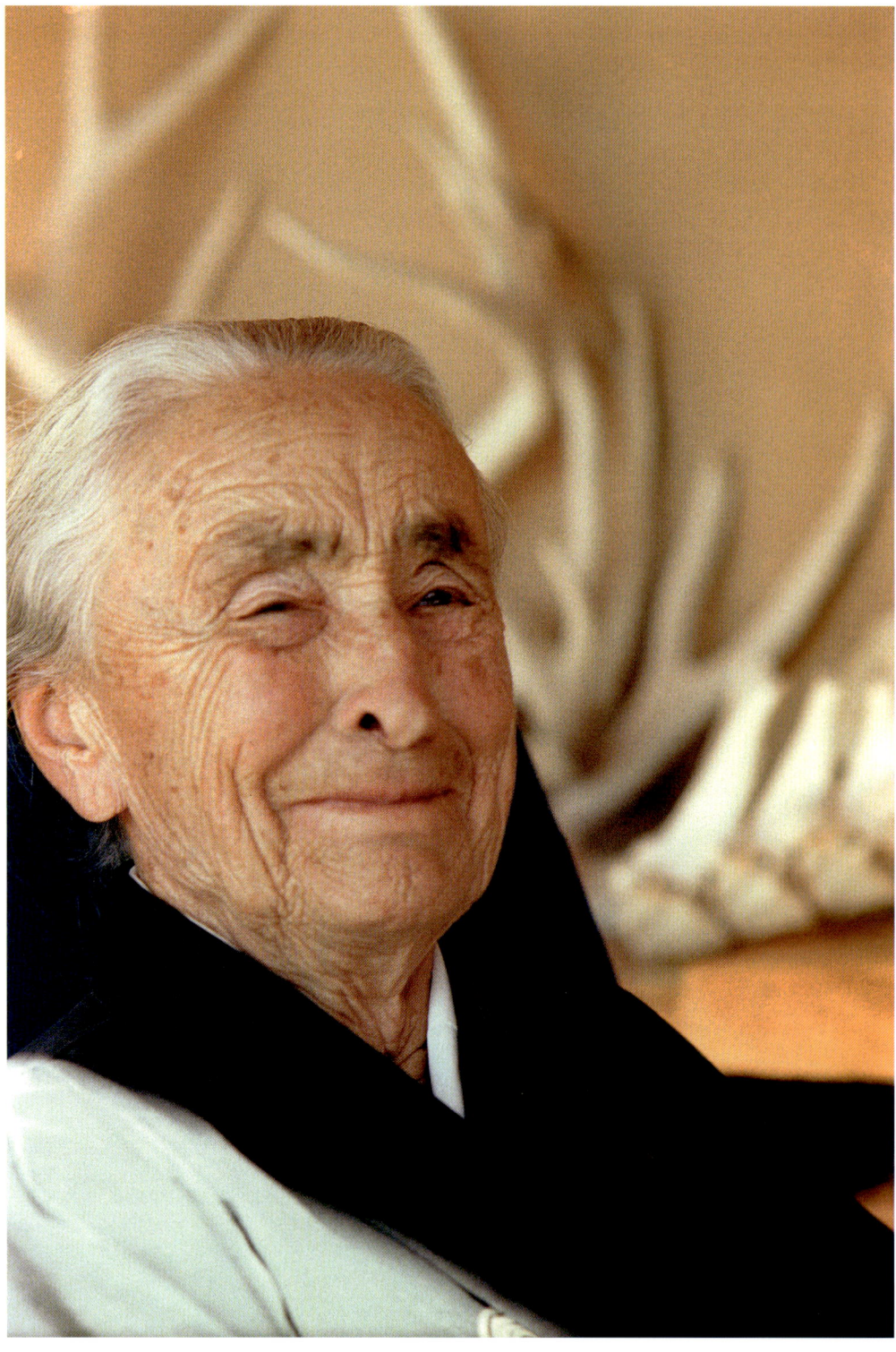

O'Keeffe sitting in the portal at Ghost Ranch, amused by something just told to her.

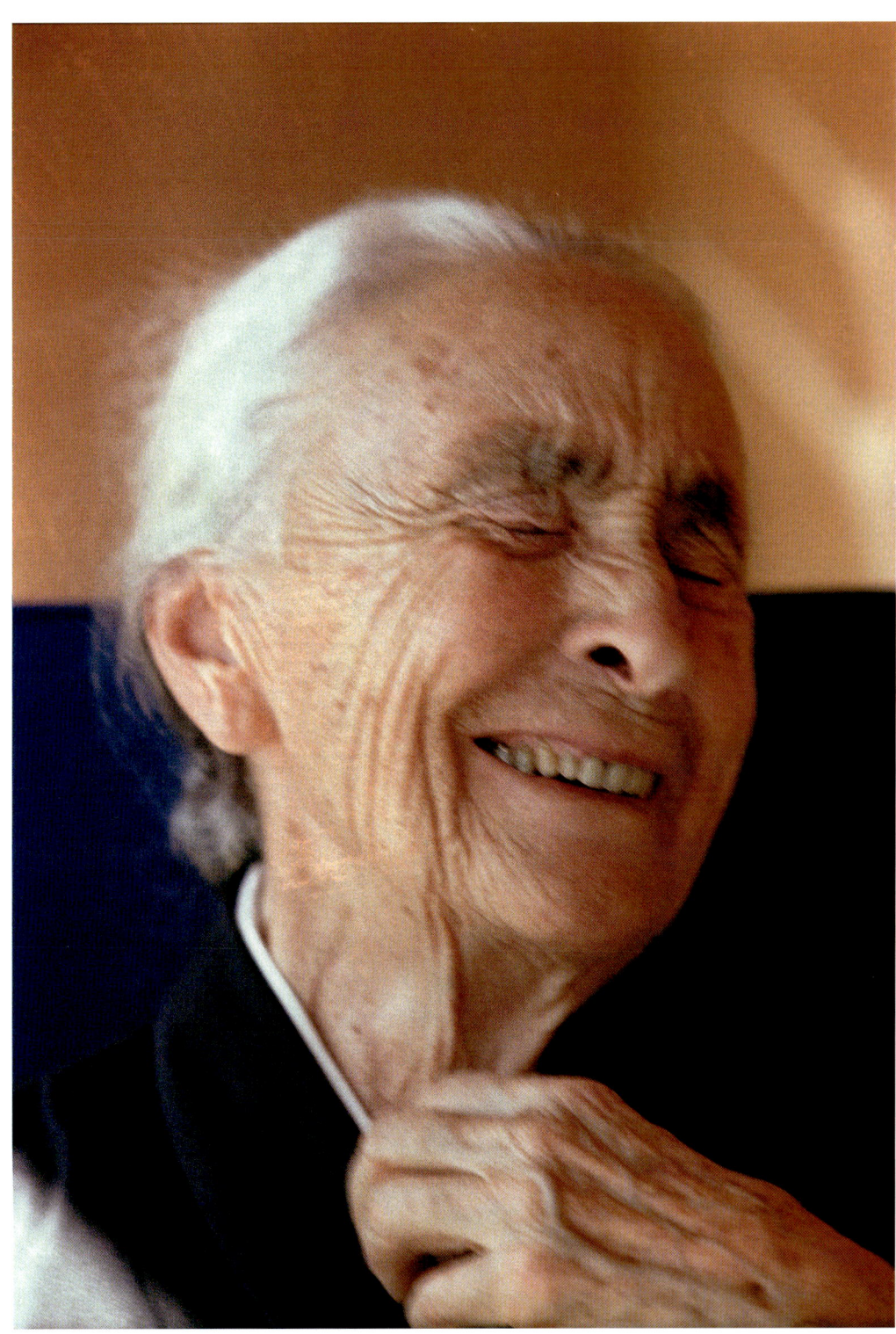

O'Keeffe laughing heartily at something in the conversation.

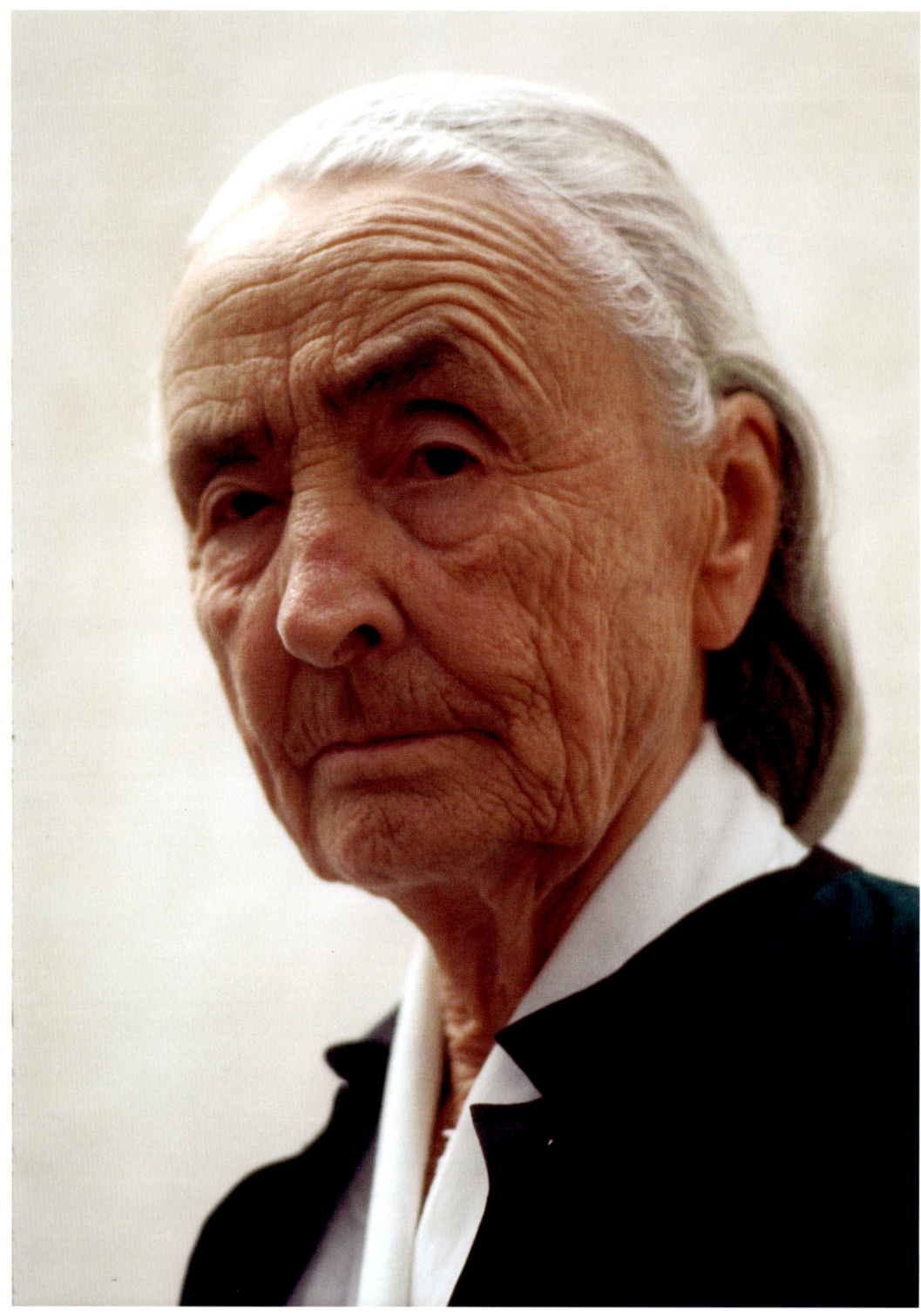

O'Keeffe in the roofless room at Abiquiú.

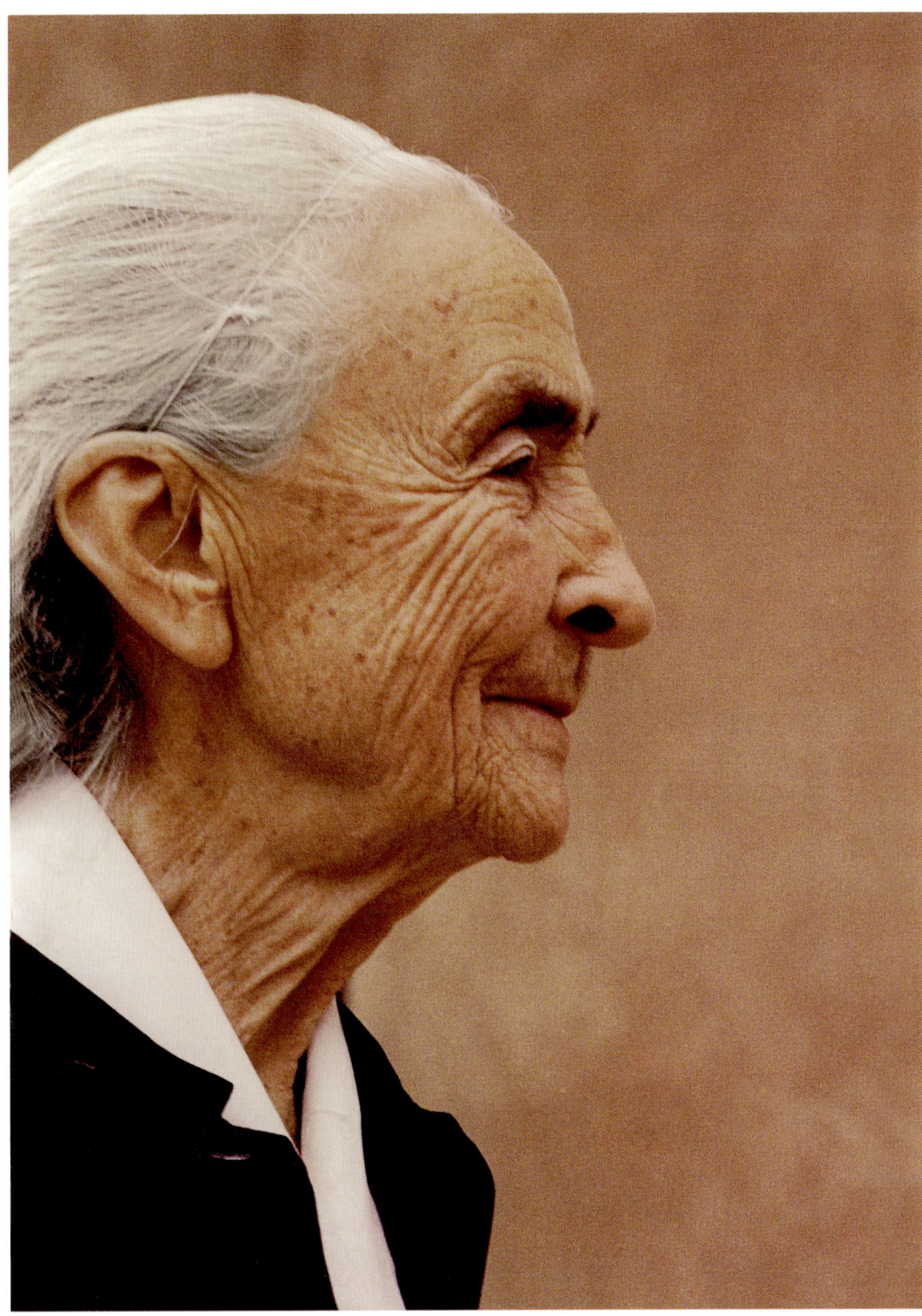

Close-up profile of O'Keeffe smiling in the sitting room at Abiquiú.

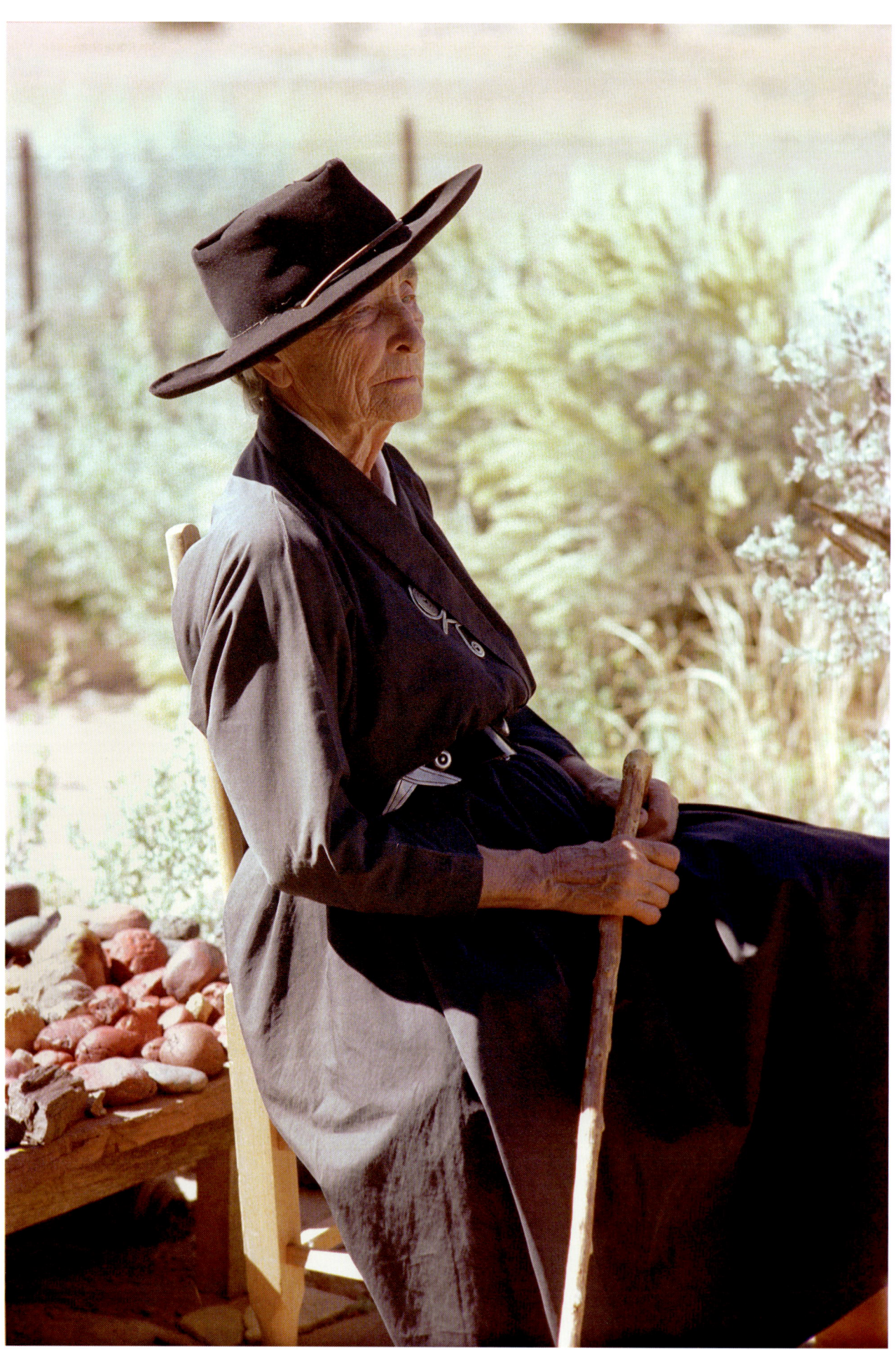

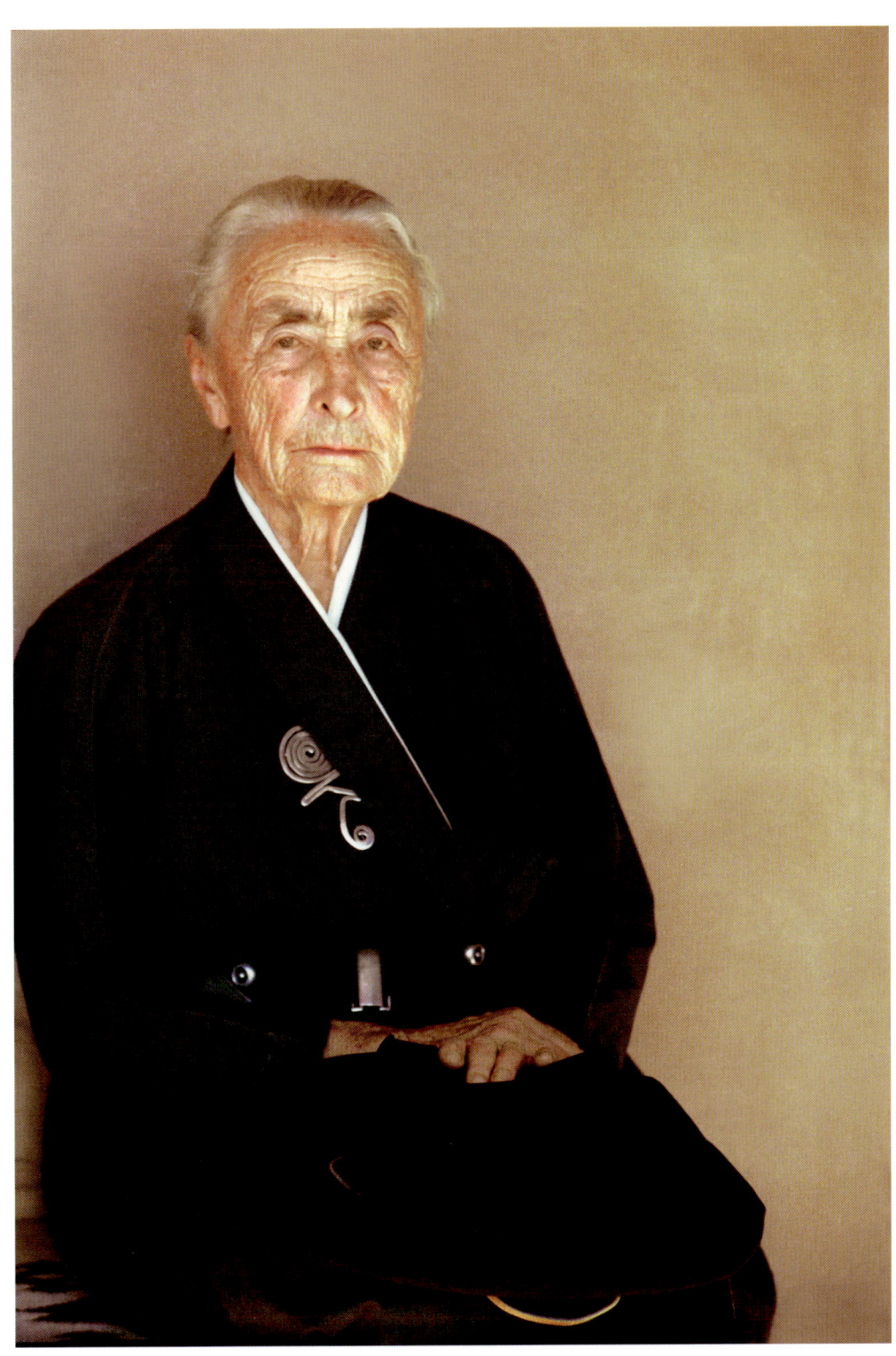

O'Keeffe in the sitting room at Abiquiú.

Opposite page: O'Keeffe relaxing in a chair next to her collection of stones in the patio at Ghost Ranch.

PART 2

Georgia O'Keeffe & Juan Hamilton

A "Strong and Tender Connection"

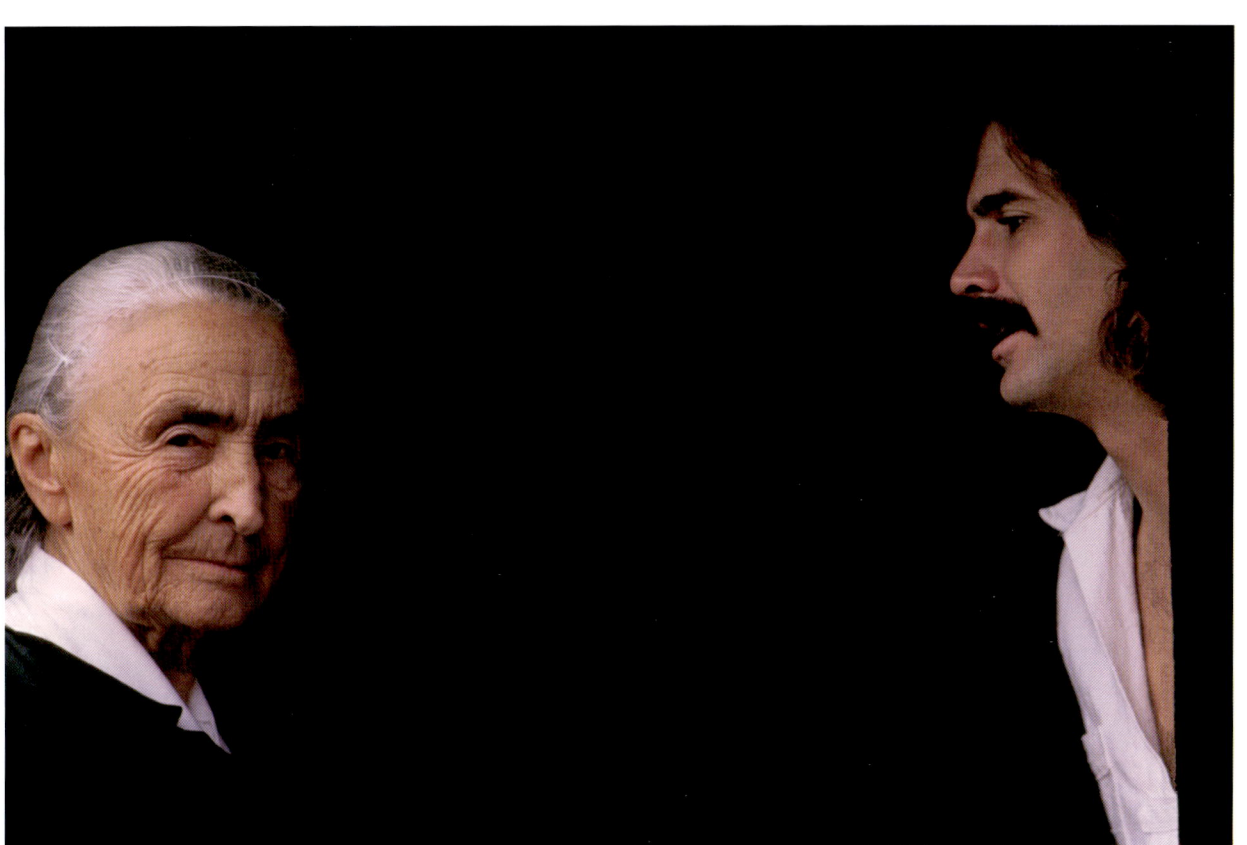

O'Keeffe and Hamilton at Abiquiú in a patio doorway.

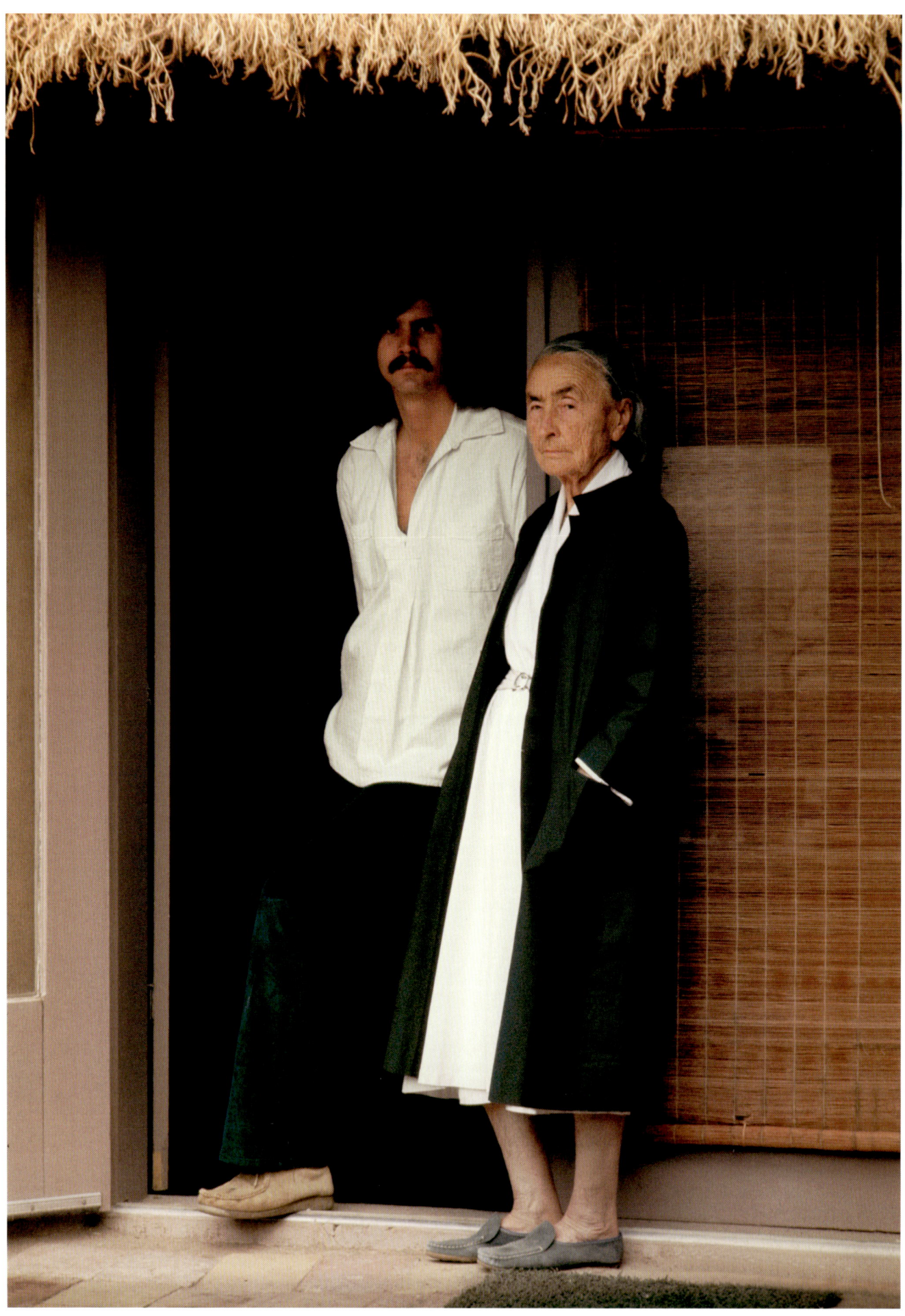

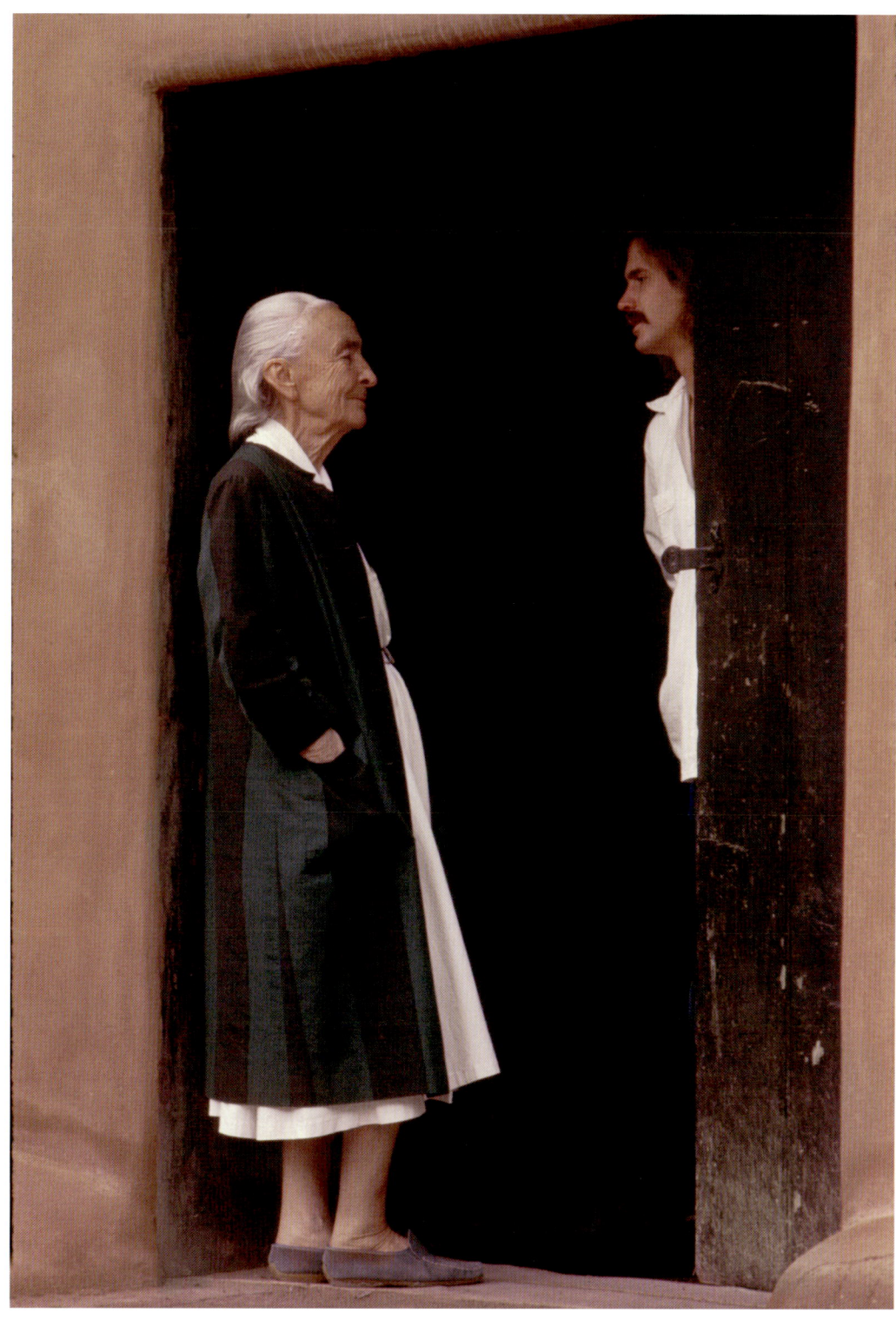

O'Keeffe and Hamilton at Abiquiú, chatting in the patio doorway to the *salita*,
a large storage room where I had set up my studio in 1977 for photographing paintings.

Opposite page: O'Keeffe and Hamilton at Abiquiú, standing
in the doorway leading from the patio into the dining room.

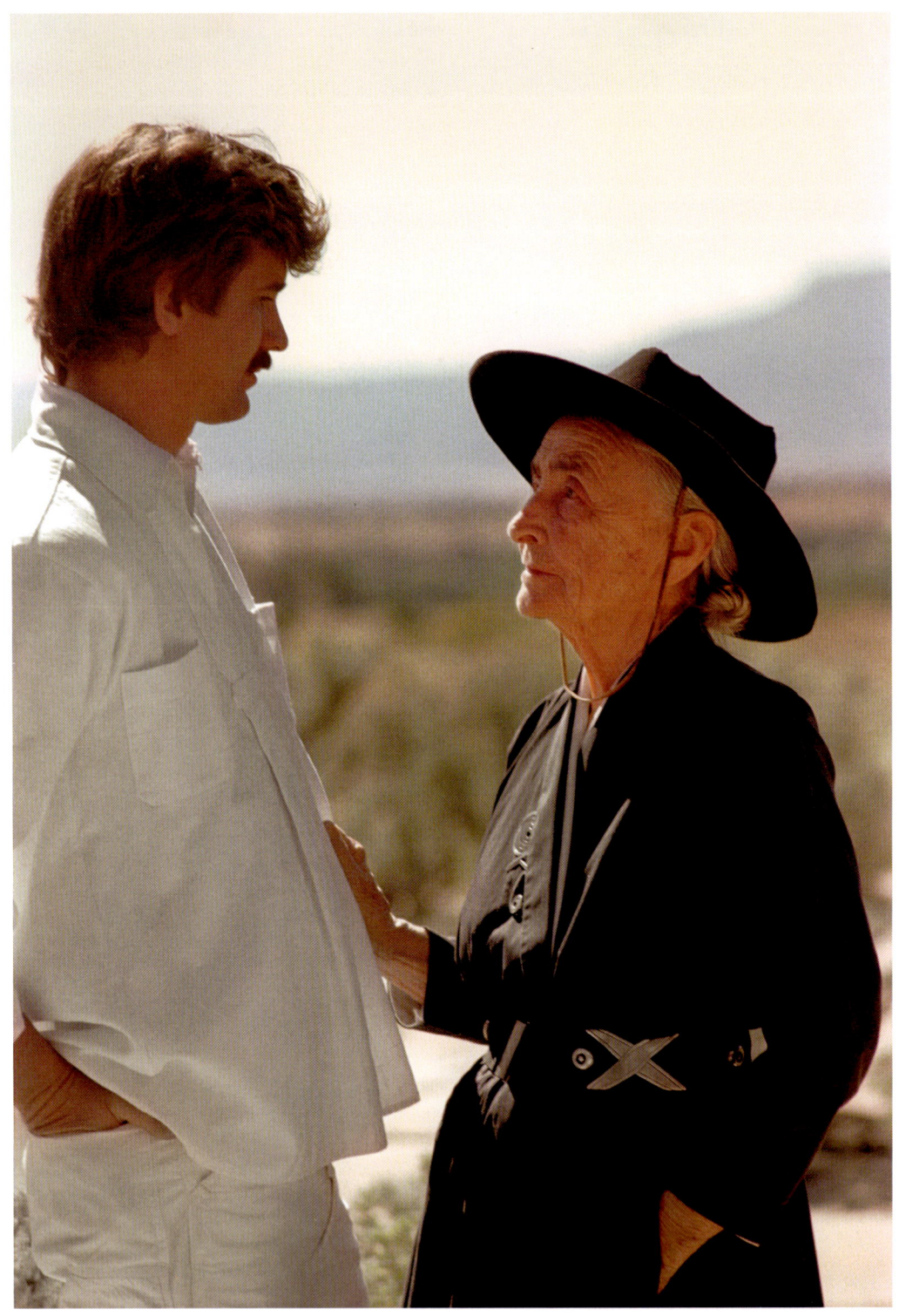

O'Keeffe and Hamilton having a serious conversation in a field at Ghost Ranch.

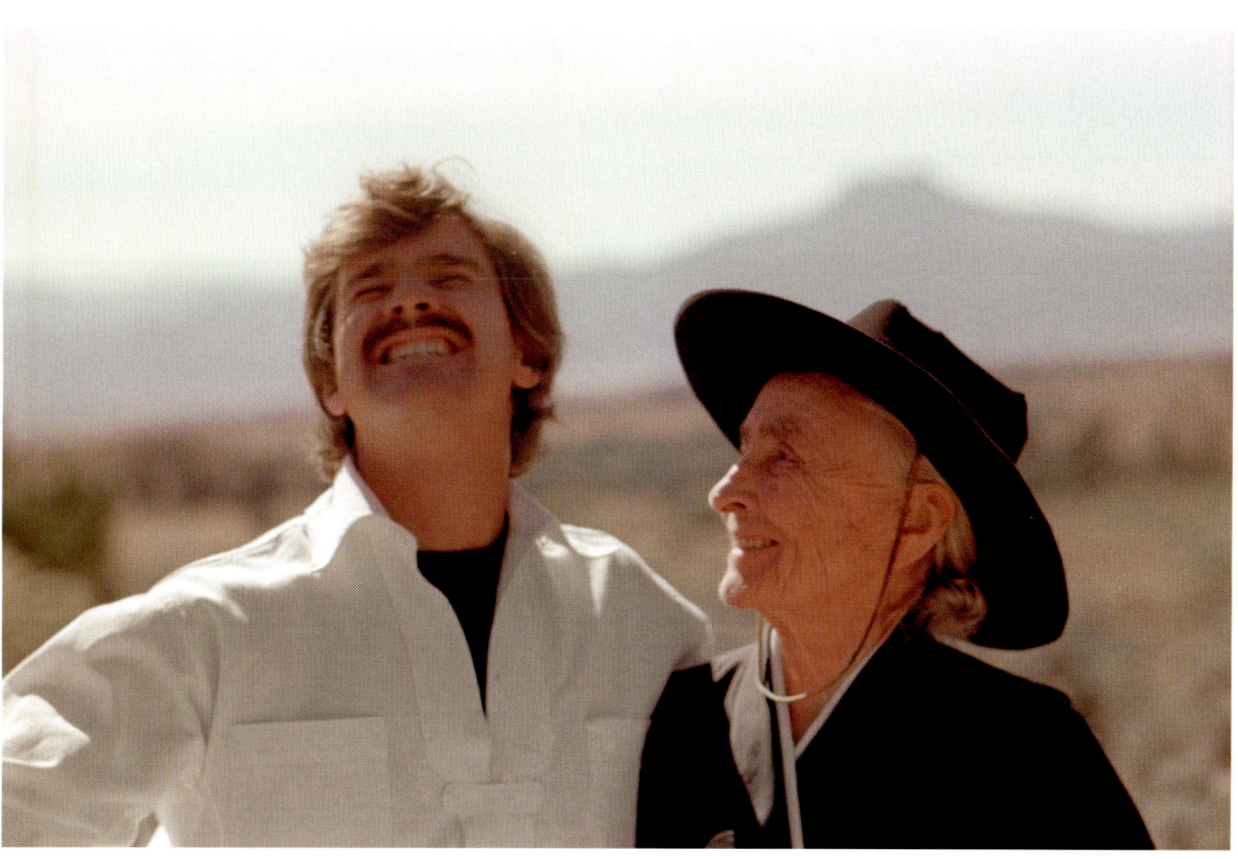

O'Keeffe and Hamilton laughing at a shared joke in a field at Ghost Ranch.
The Pedernal is the bluish mountain in the background.

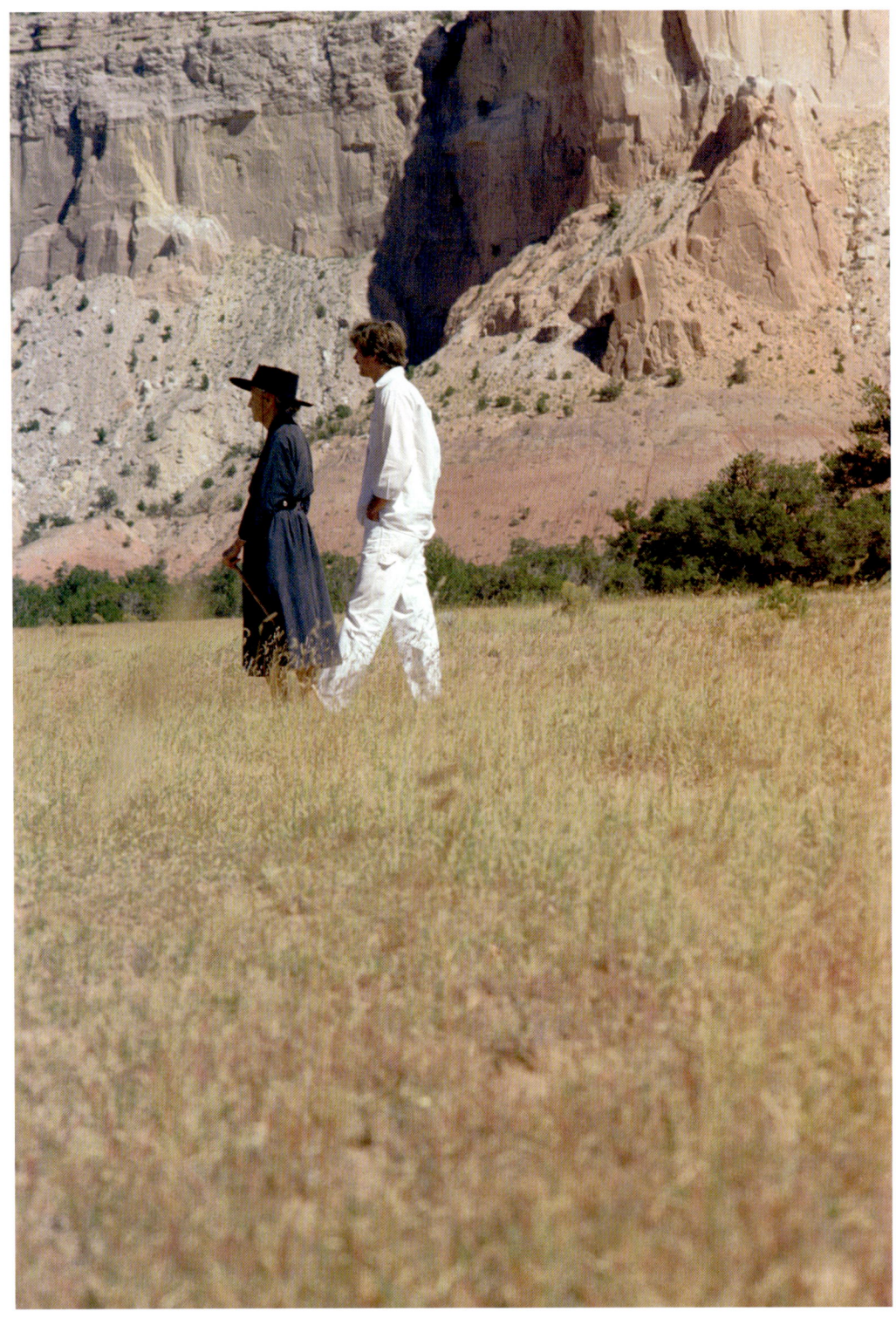

O'Keeffe and Hamilton strolling in the fields at Ghost Ranch.

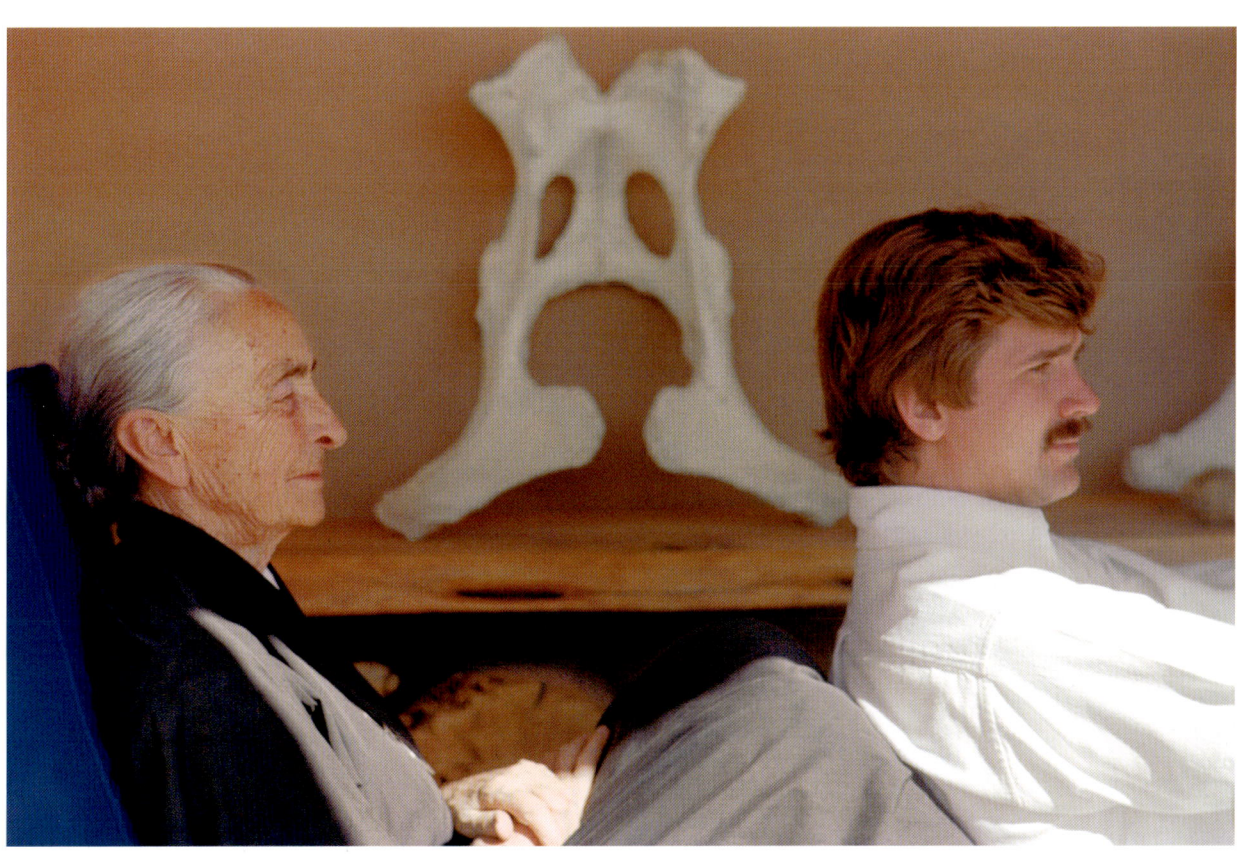

O'Keeffe and Hamilton relaxing in the portal of the patio at Ghost Ranch.

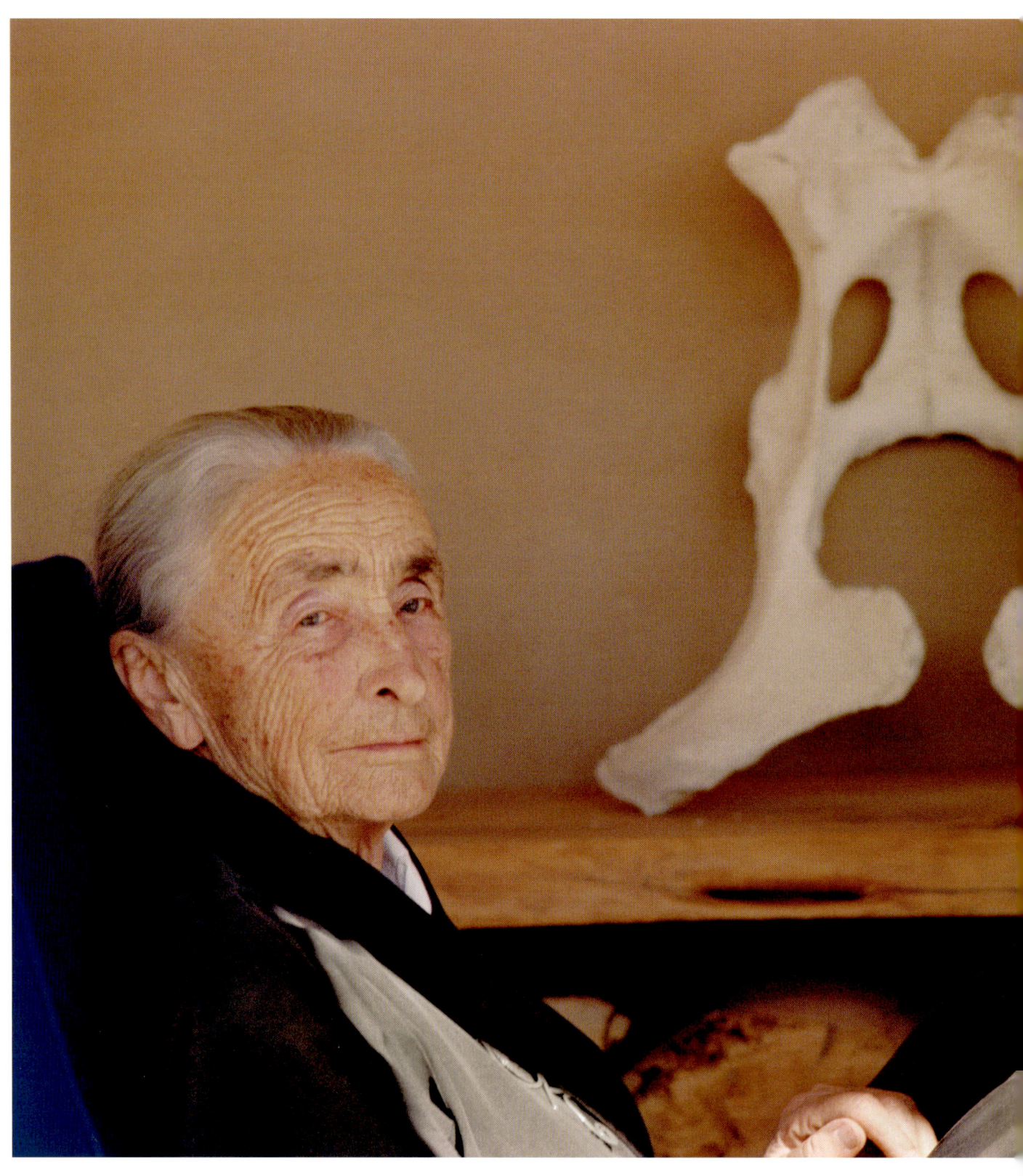

O'Keeffe and Hamilton facing the camera in the patio portal at Ghost Ranch.

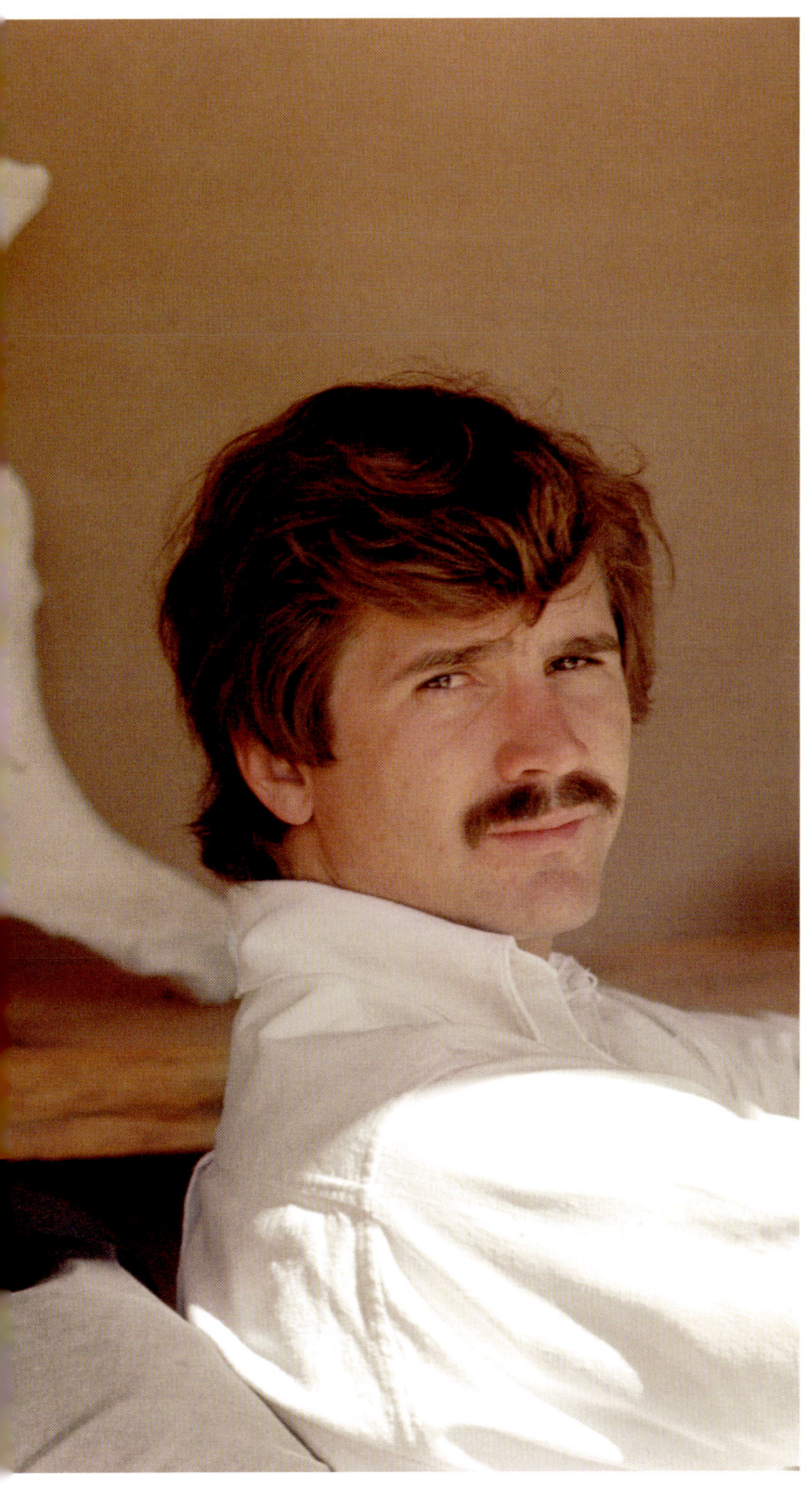

43

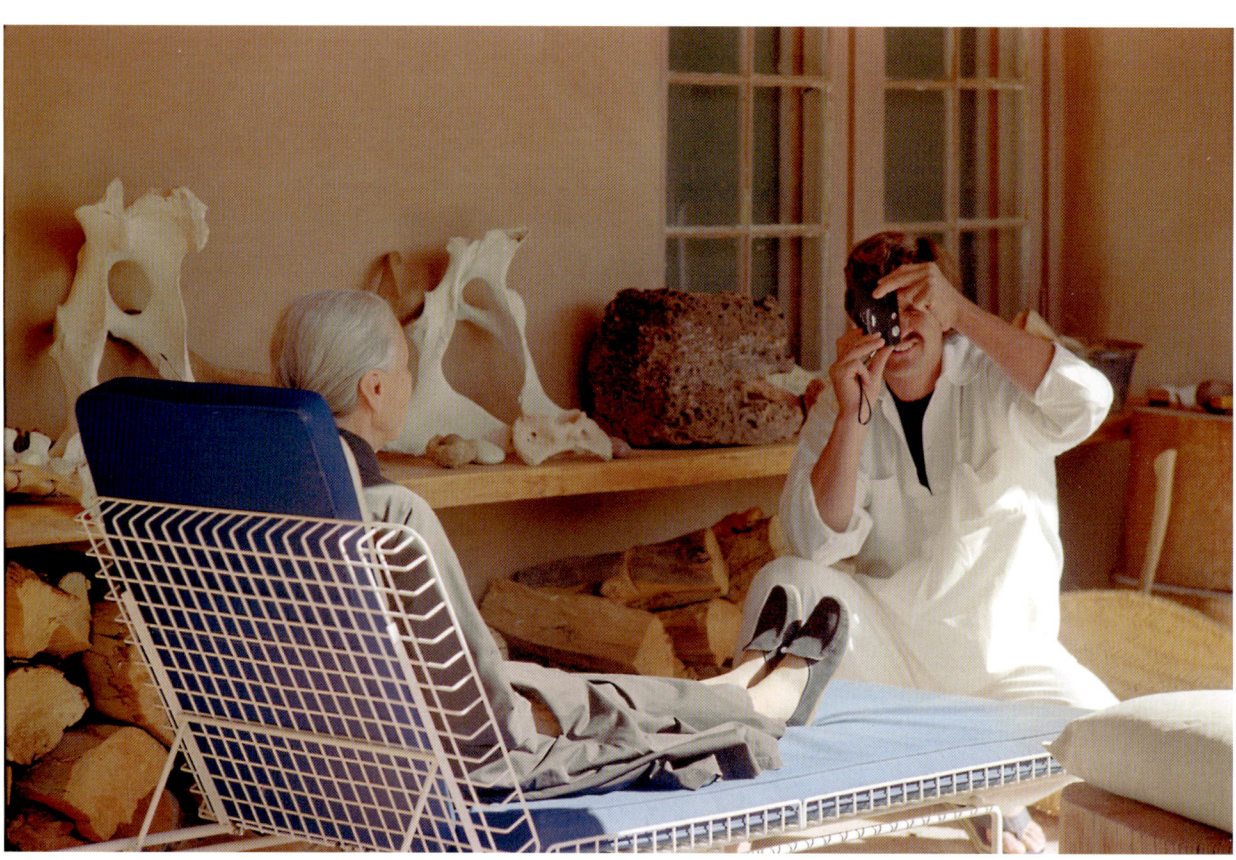

Hamilton taking photos while lounging in the portal of the patio at Ghost Ranch.
Hamilton is photographing me photographing him and O'Keeffe.

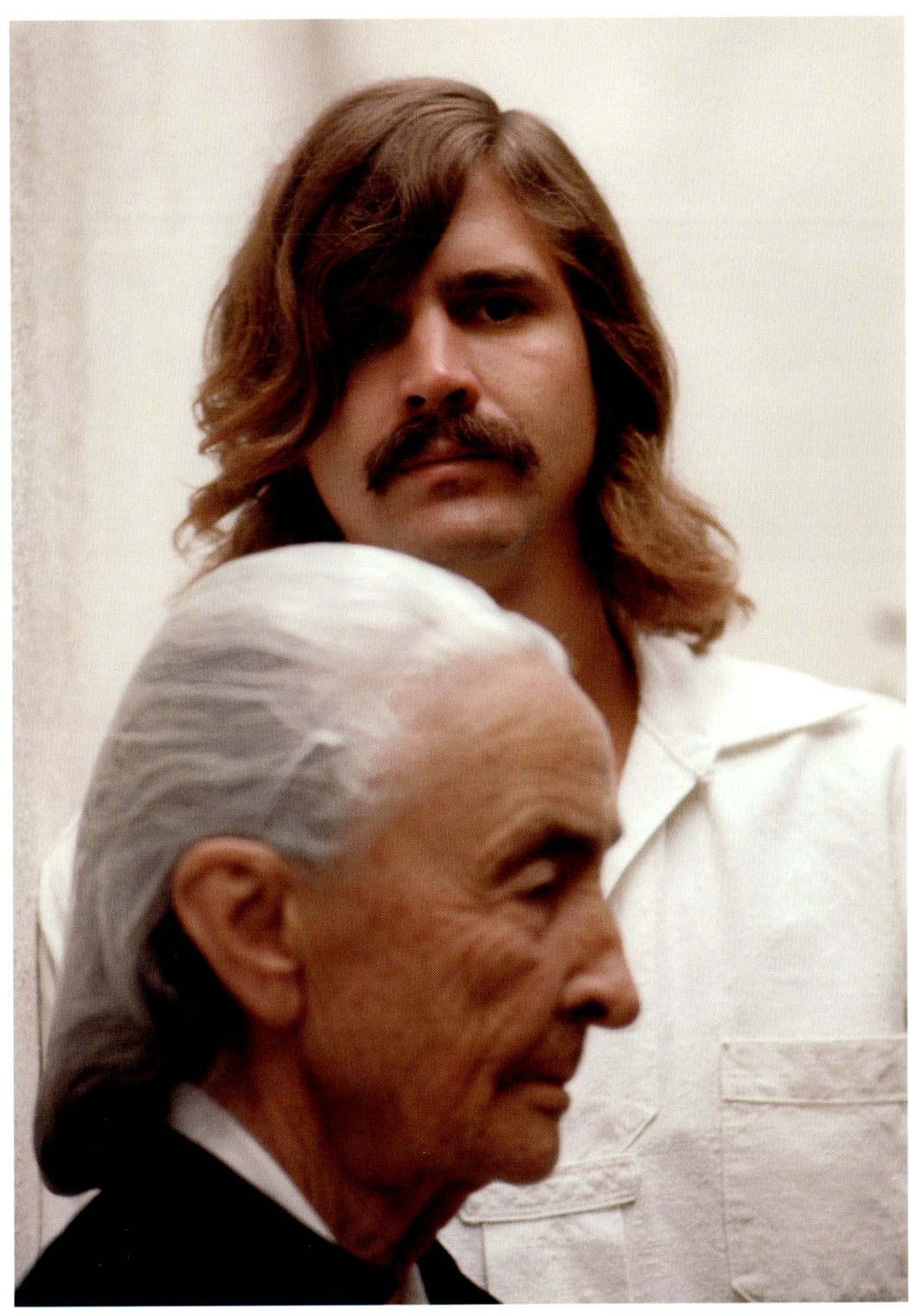

O'Keeffe and Hamilton in Abiquiú. This photo was taken in the roofless room.

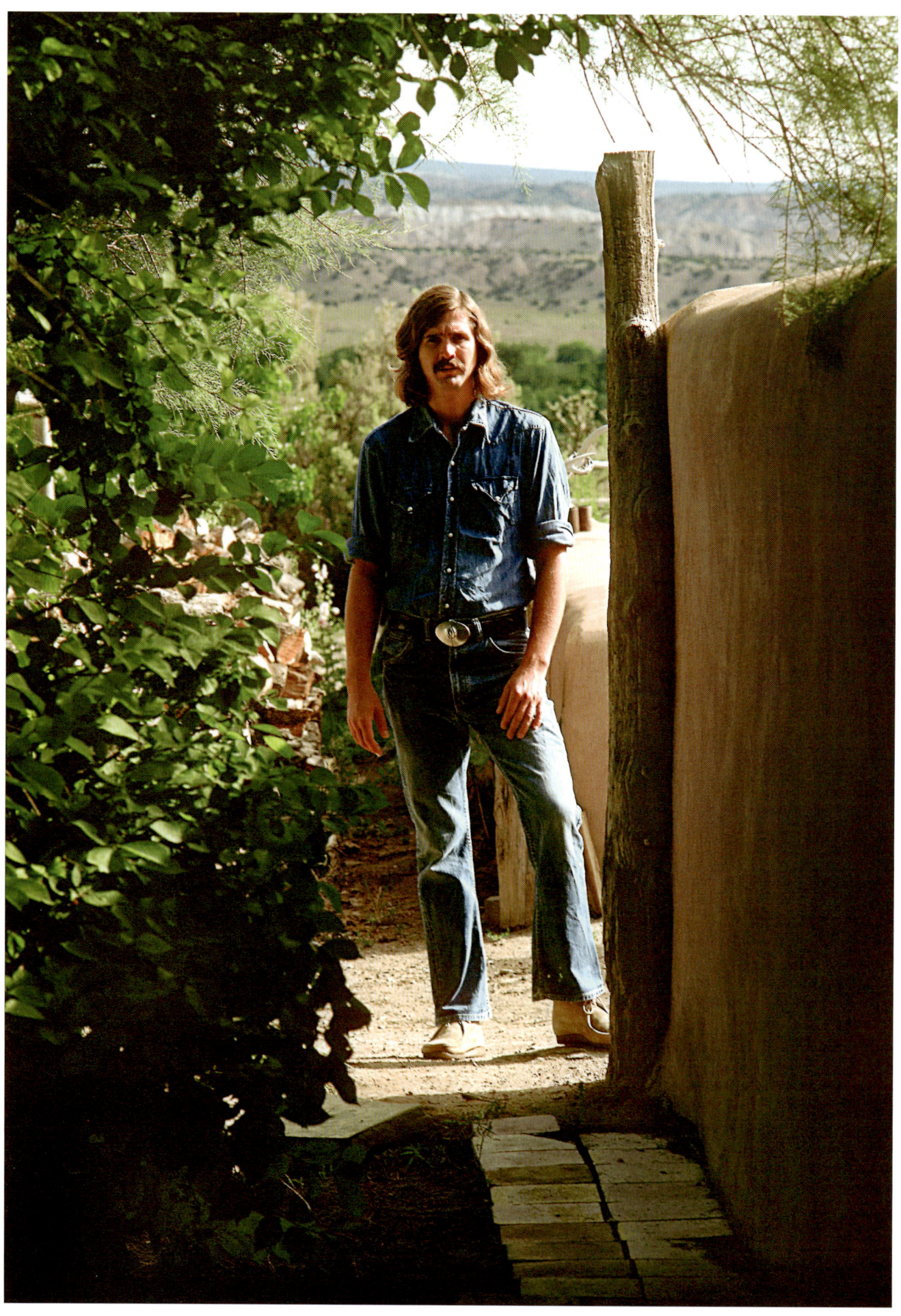

PART 3

Her Space

*The Places and People
Important to Georgia O'Keeffe*

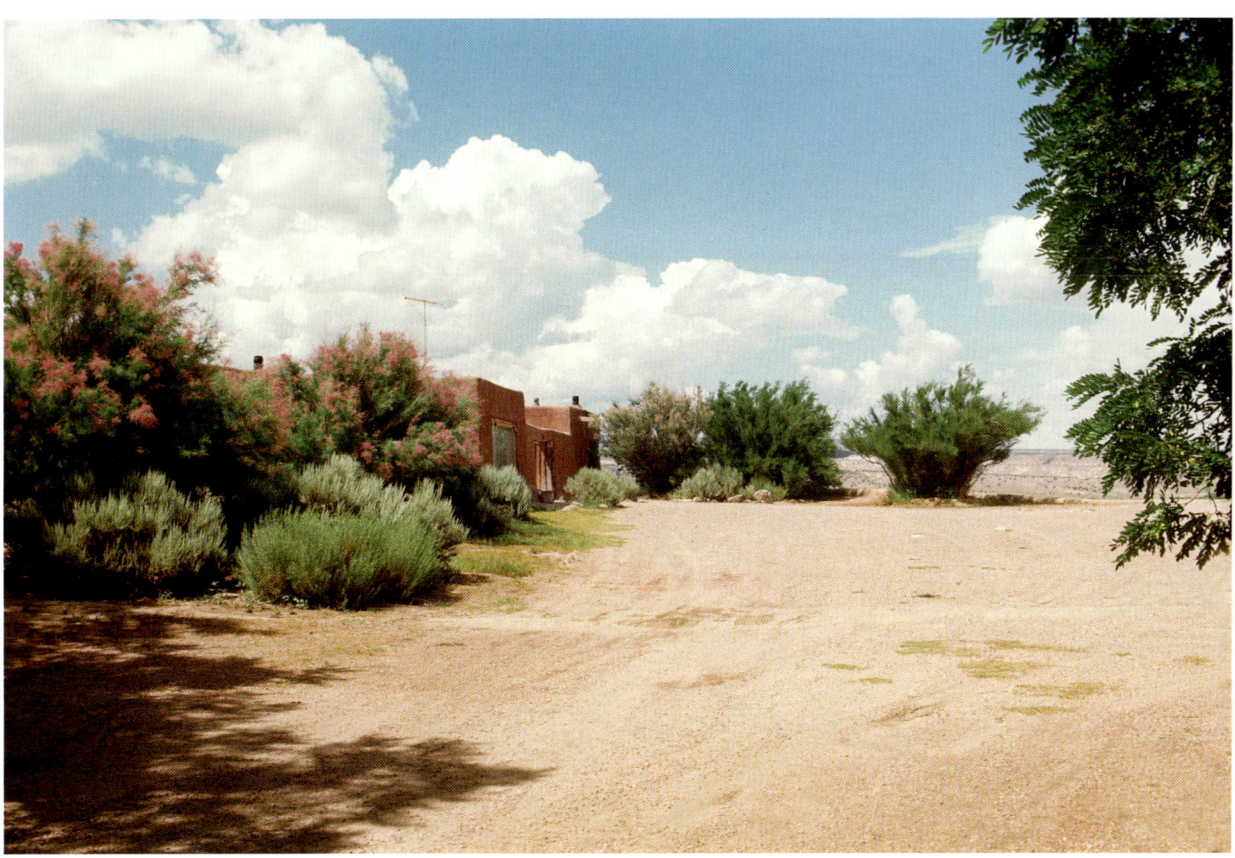

Front entrance to the Abiquiú house. This view is facing north with the edge of the yard
overlooking the Chama Valley. I always had a feeling when passing through this entrance that
I was emerging into a world, O'Keeffe's world, where aesthetic sensibility and beauty reigned supreme.

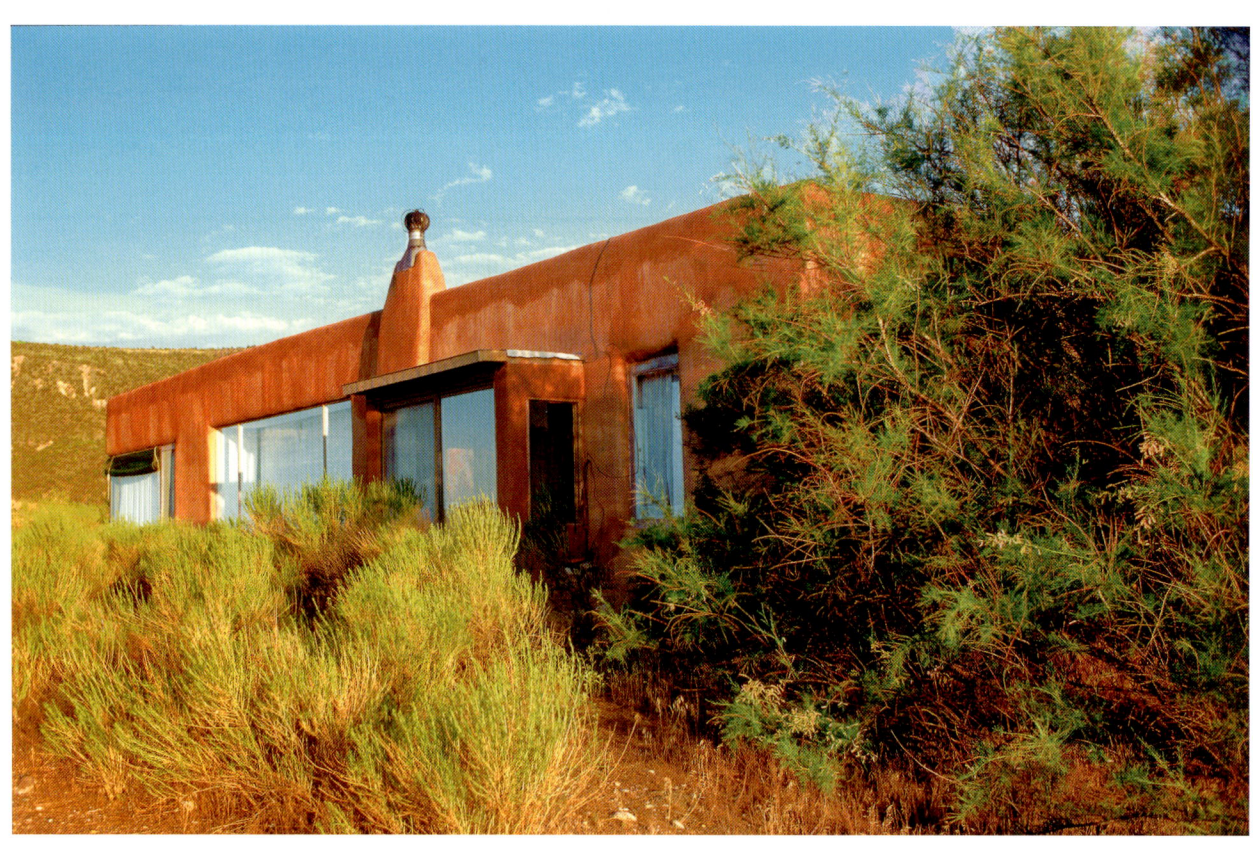

Outside wall and large north-facing windows of O'Keeffe's
Abiquiú studio bathed in the late-afternoon sunlight.

Opposite page: When crossing the patio one day with my photo equipment on my way to my makeshift
studio, I noticed what looked like a shed but is actually the main entrance to the Abiquiú house as seen
from inside. The arrangement of firewood, the ceramic bowl, the antlers, the closed door with light
coming through the cracks, the vigas, and a single hanging lightbulb made such an interesting still life that
I had to stop and set up my 8 × 10 camera to shoot it. I didn't know at the time that other photographers
before me had been equally captivated by this sight and produced well-known photos of it.

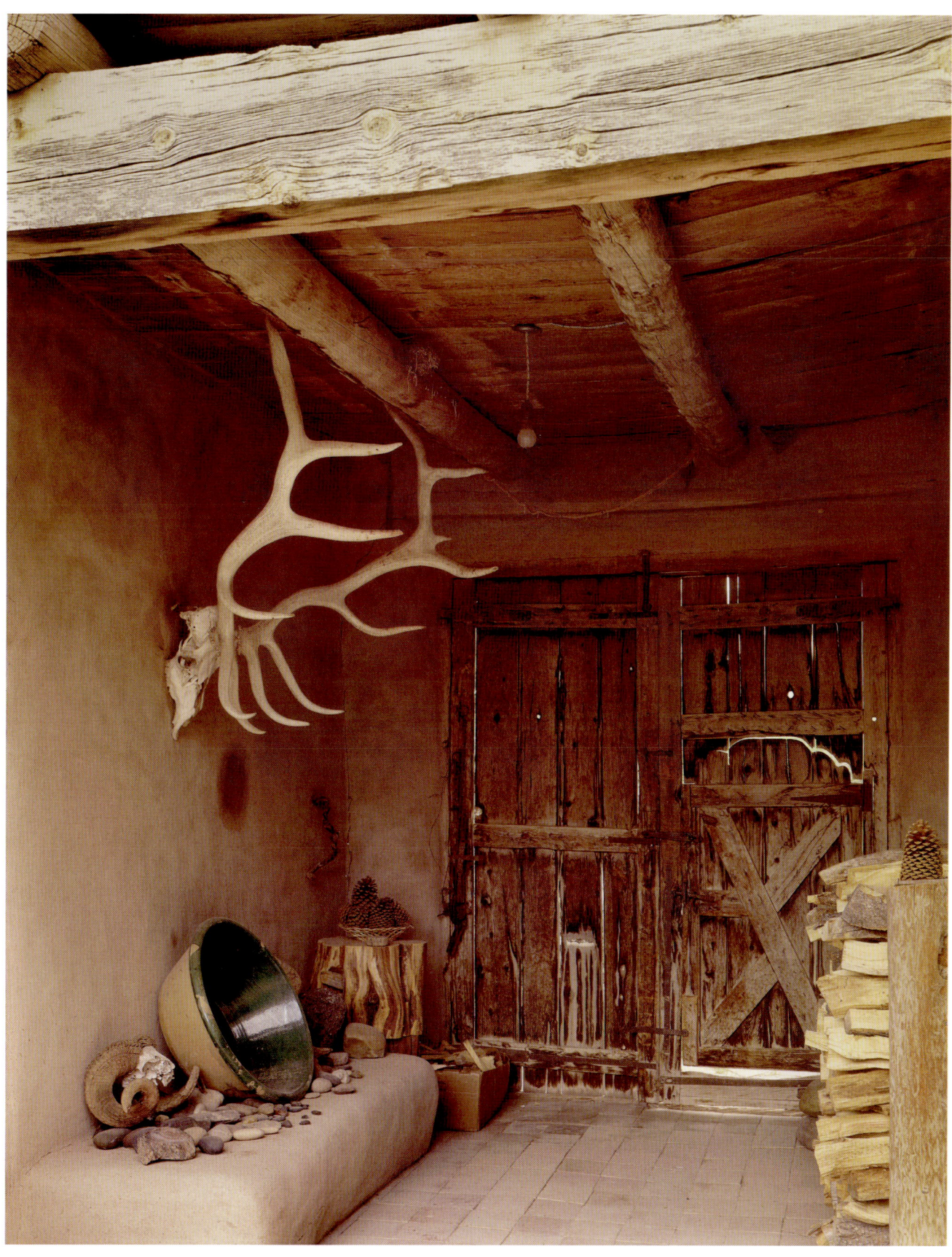

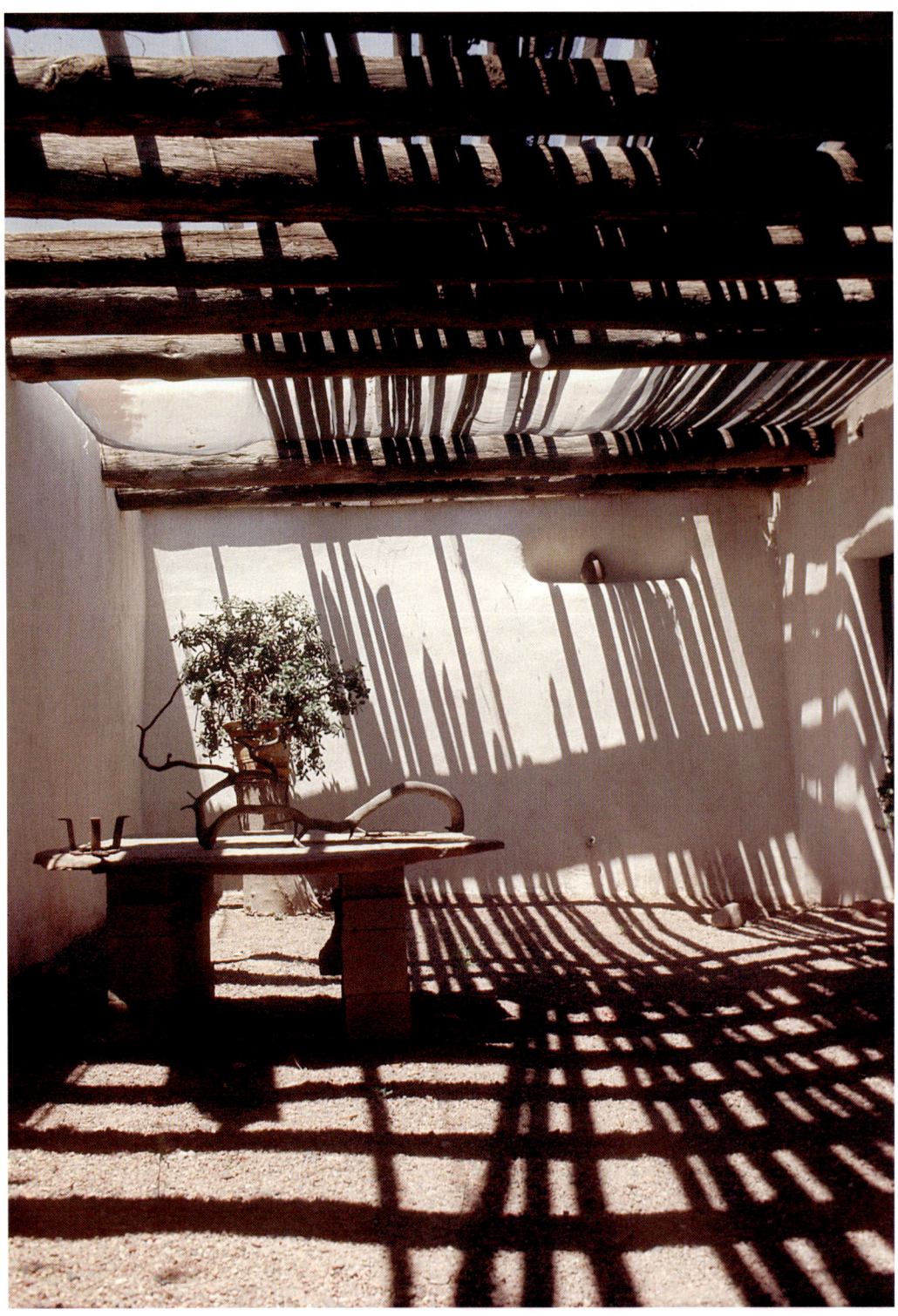

54

This room is called the "roofless room." It is the only room in the Abiquiú compound that has no roof, only vigas with thin, hand-carved logs crossing them intermittently, allowing sunlight to enter and create striking patterns of shadows on the floor and walls.

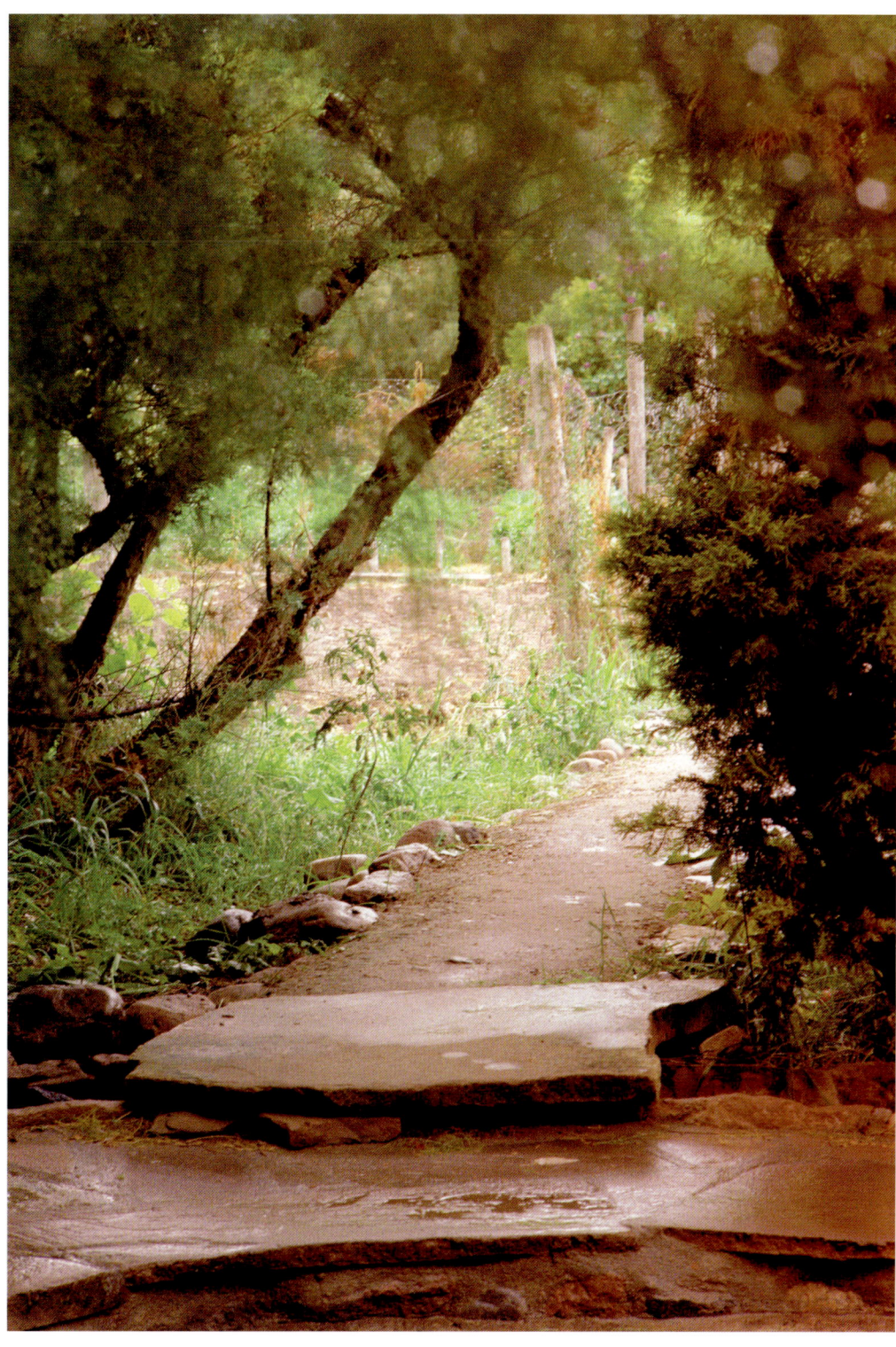

Walkway of flagstone steps and entrance to the garden
where O'Keeffe grew vegetables, herbs, fruits, and flowers.

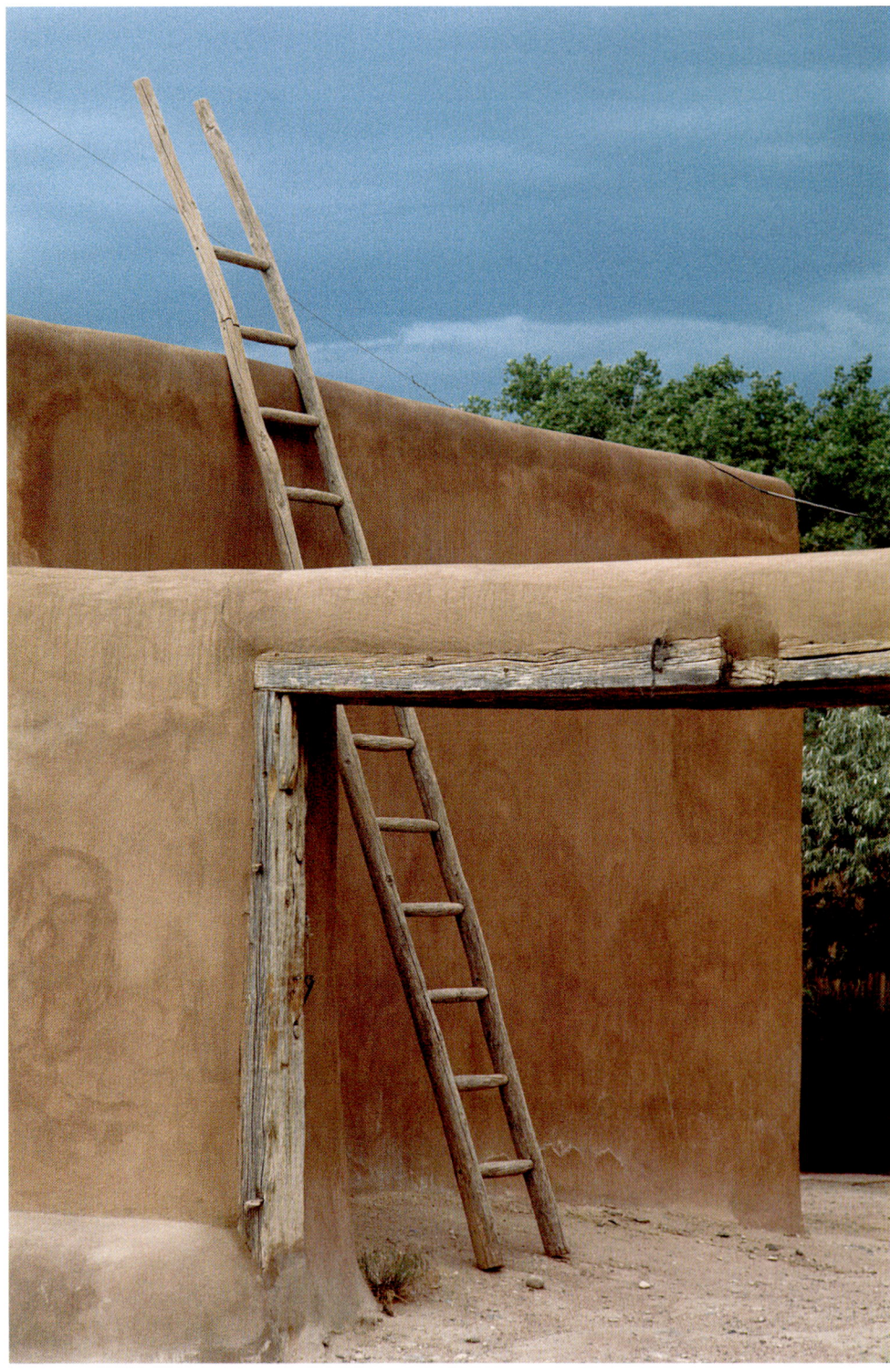

Pueblo-style hand-hewn log ladder, sometimes called a kiva ladder, resting against an adobe wall in the interior space of the Abiquiú house. These types of ladders were used by the ancient Southwestern Native American peoples to access the roofs and upper floors of their adobe and cliff dwellings.

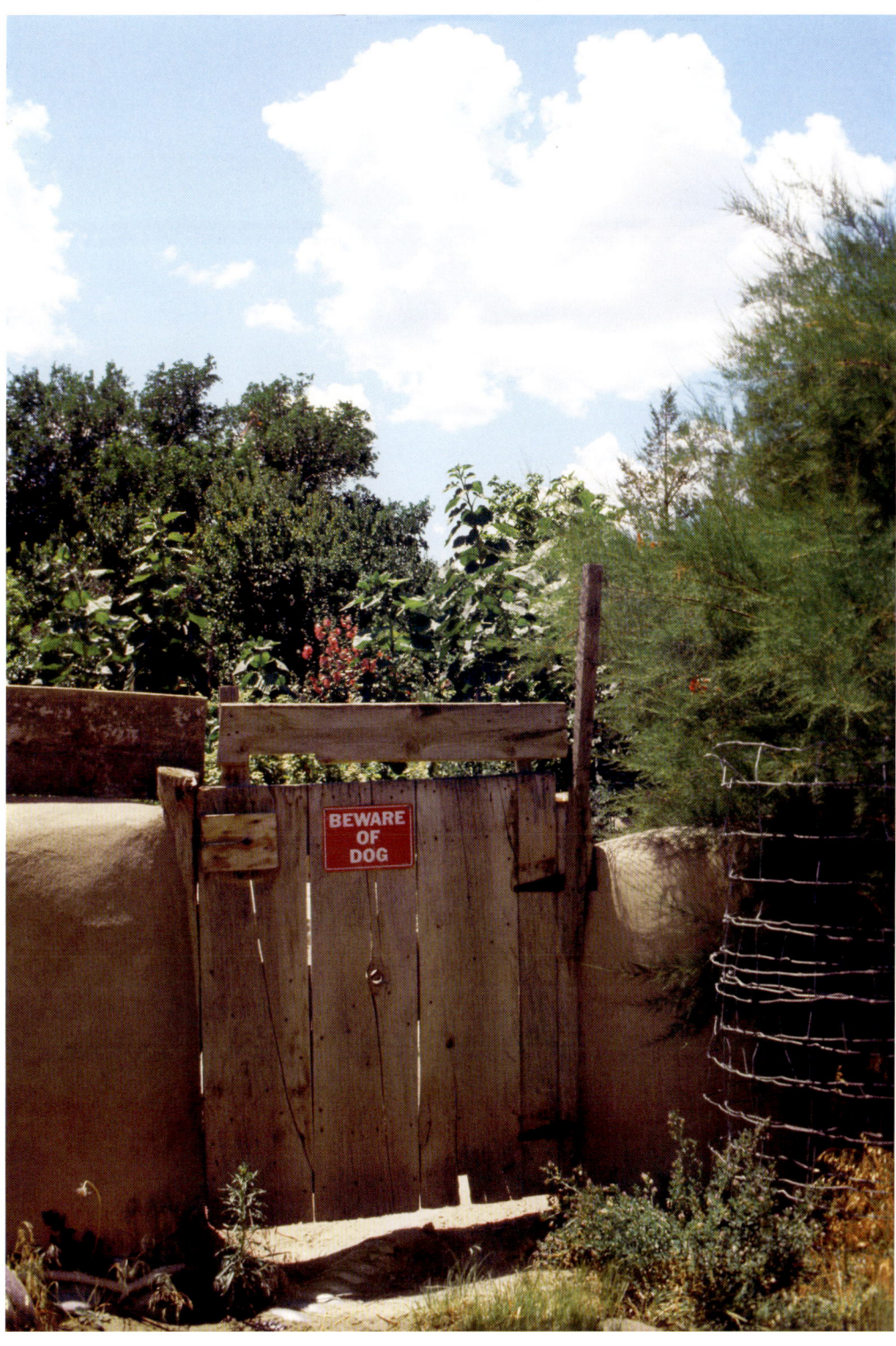

One of the entrances to the vegetable and flower garden in the Abiquiú house. The "Beware of Dog" sign is one of several on the various entrance gates to parts of the complex. Coming from a very urban background where "Beware of" signs were usually seen on the outside of closed shops or warehouses, I at first found these signs odd in the context of the beautiful and benign surroundings in which they were displayed.

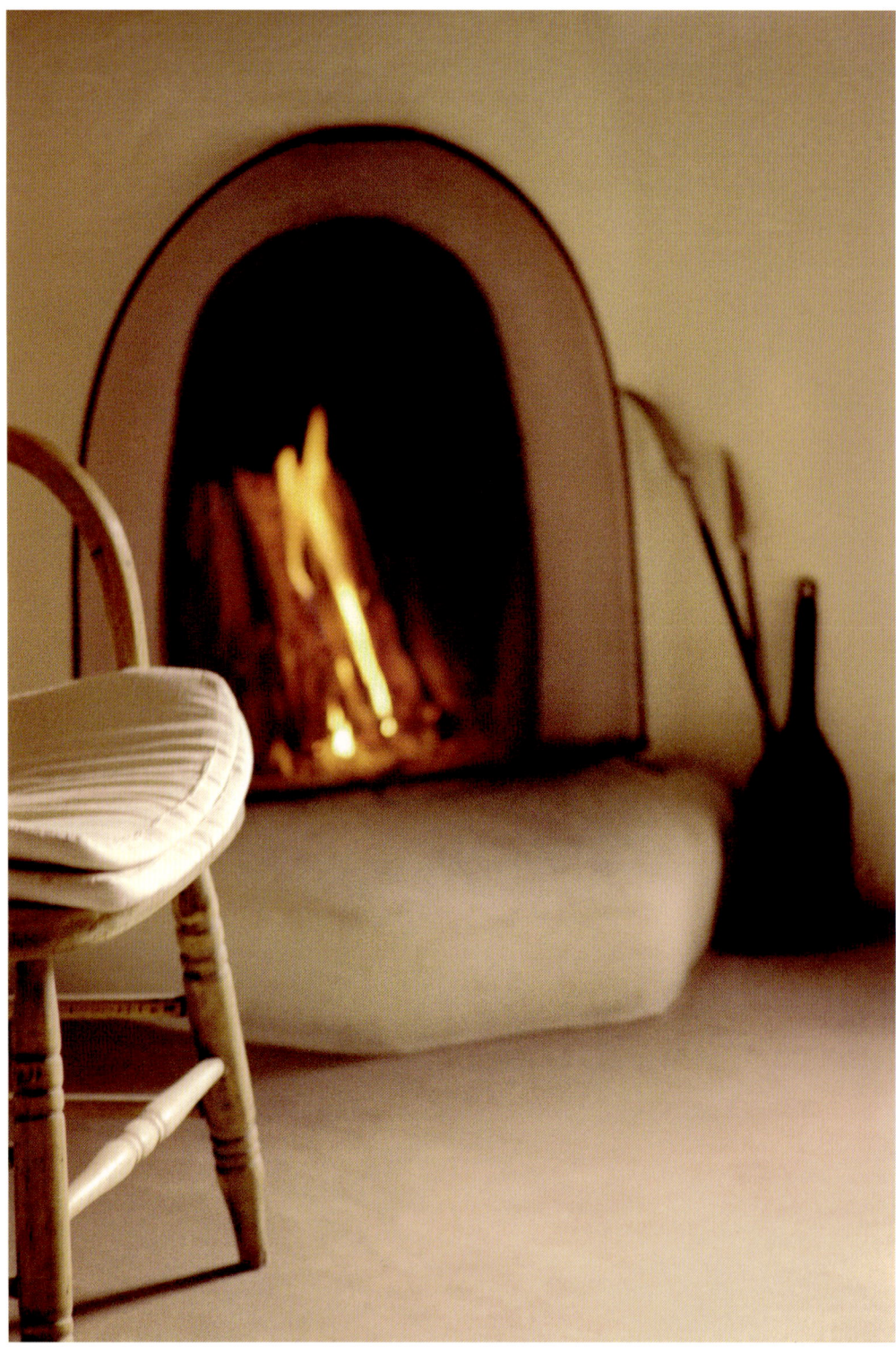

A fireplace in the Abiquiú dining room. This is a typical fireplace design in traditional adobe houses.

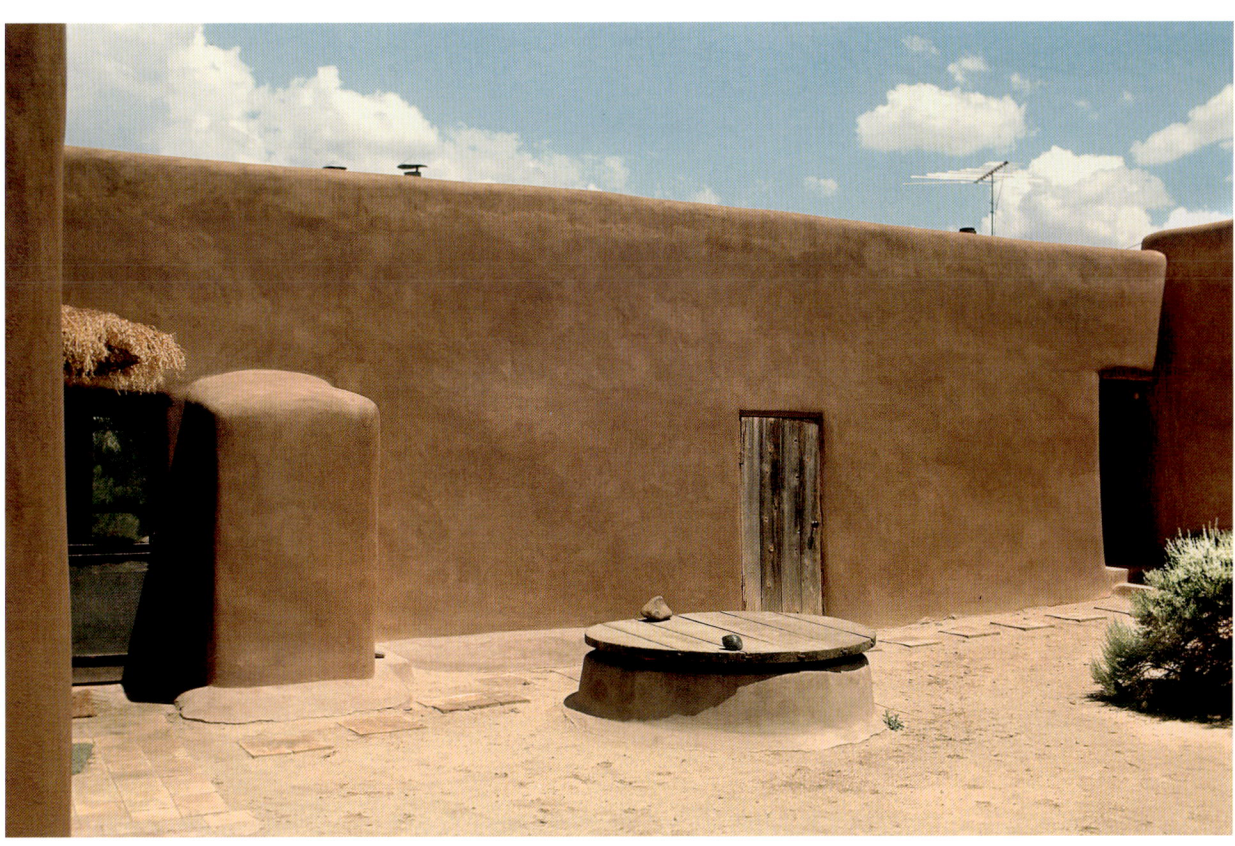

Patio with doors to the *salita* (center) and the library (left) as well as an entranceway to the garden of the Abiquiú house (far end). In the foreground is a well with a wooden cover held down by stones. The well was used for drinking water until 1948, when indoor plumbing using municipal water was installed.

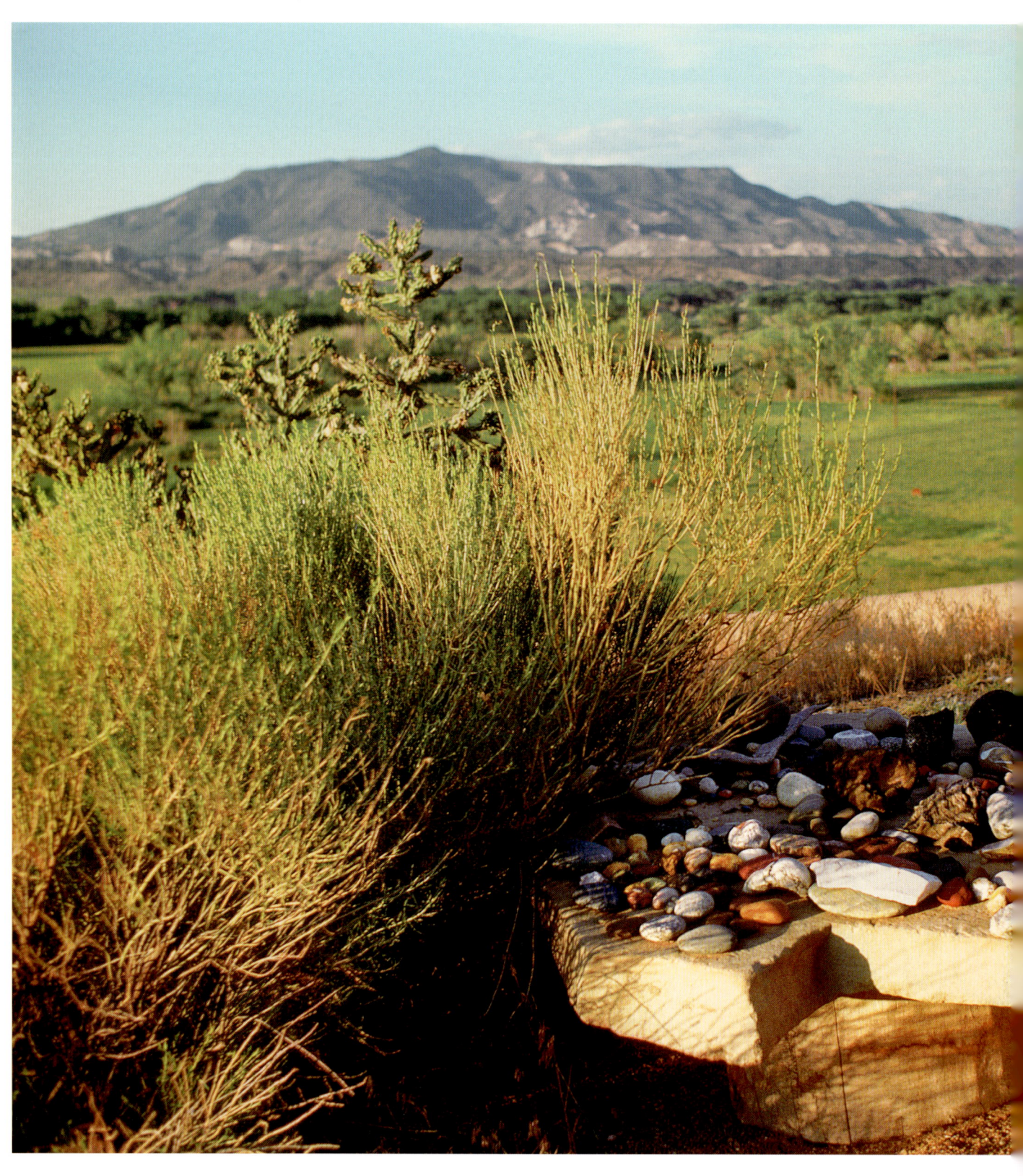

Some of O'Keeffe's rock collection outside the window to her studio in Abiquiú.
In the distance is a view of the Chama Valley, the Carson National Forest, and Black Mountain.

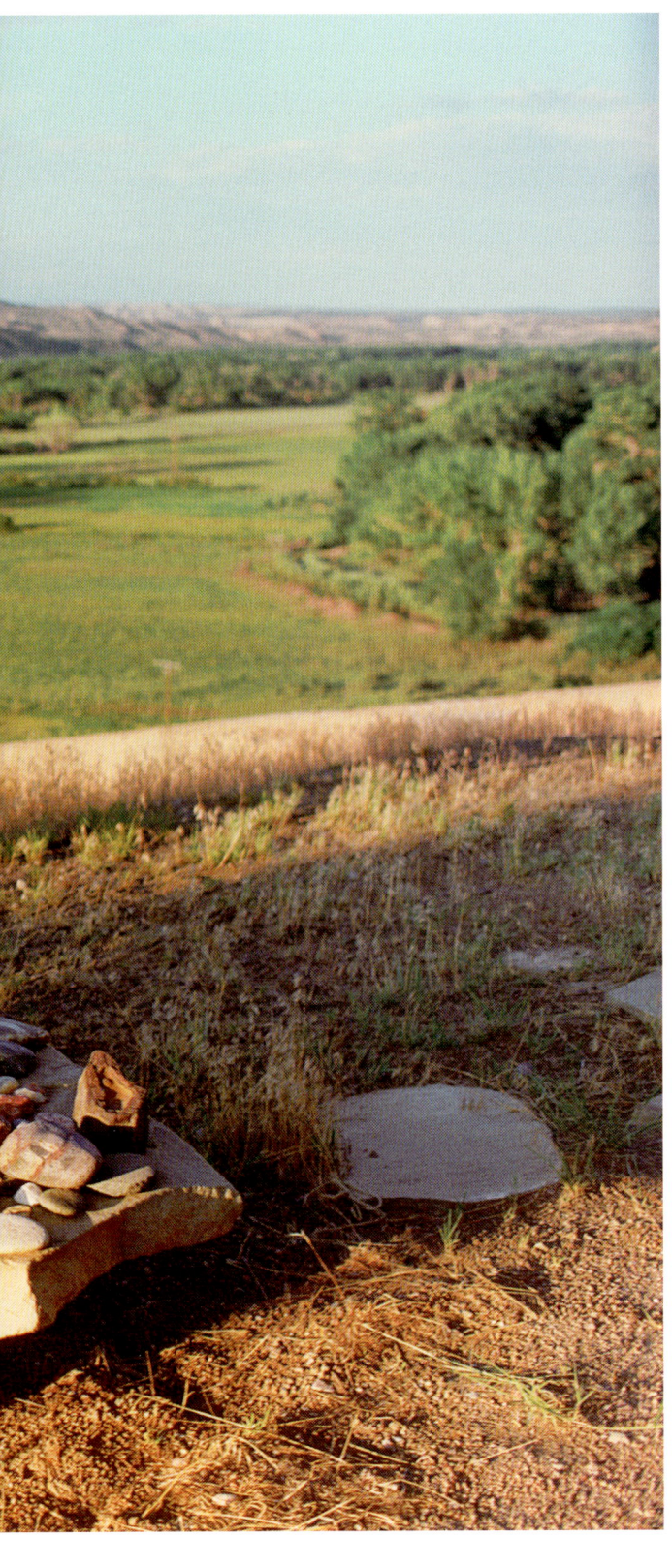

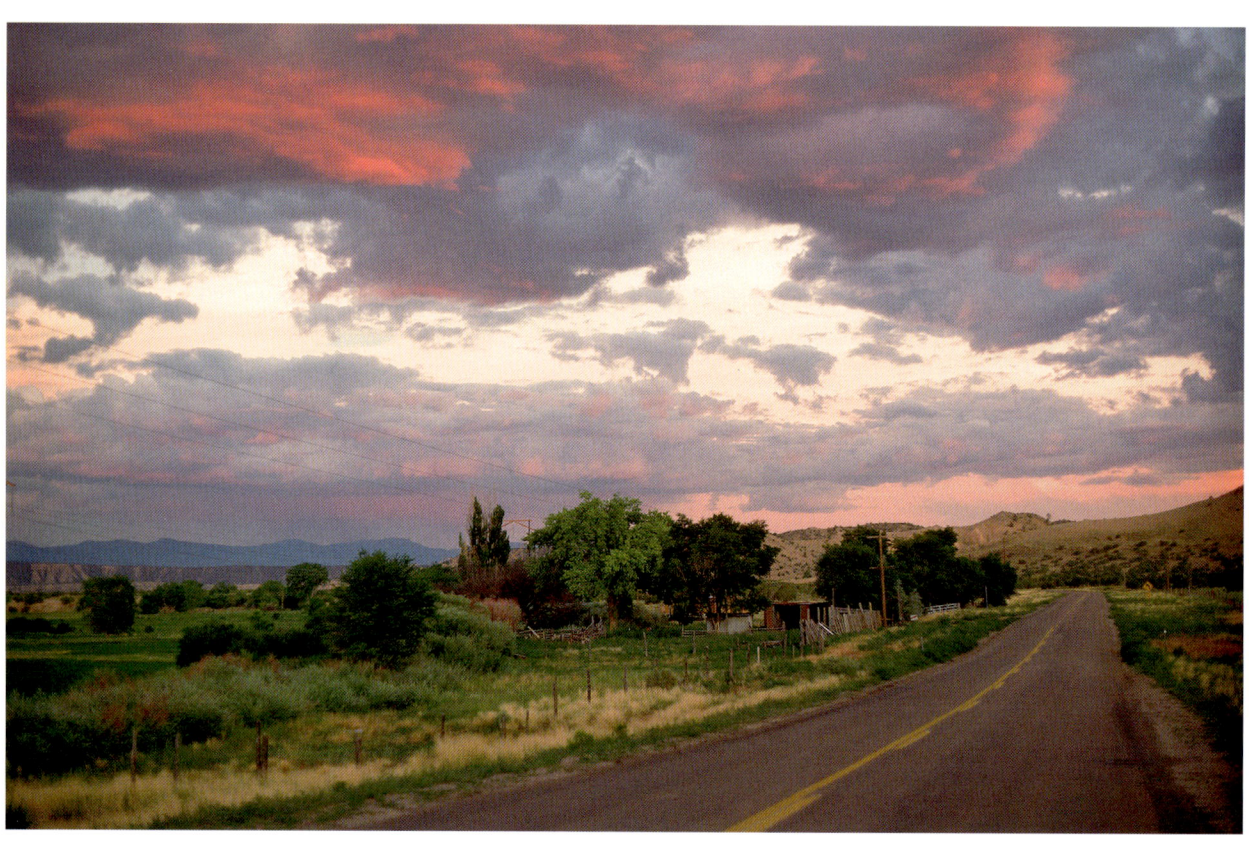

62

Sunset in the Chama Valley on the road between Santa Fe and Abiquiú.

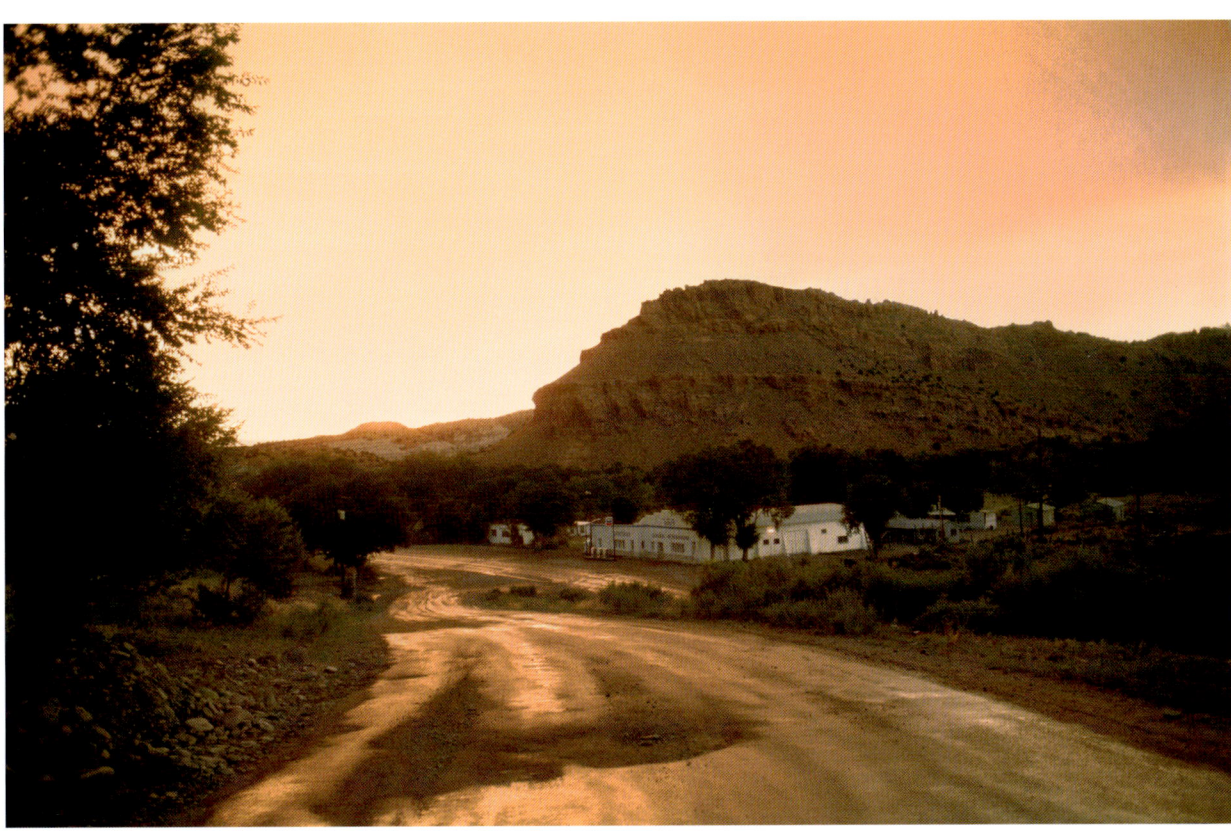

Road coming down a small hill from Abiquiú. It was sunset and had just rained, turning the road into a stream of gold. At the bottom of the hill the road connects to Route I-84, on the other side of which can be seen the group of small, white buildings comprising Bode's General Store. Bode's has been in this location since the 1890s and caters to the local population as a supply source for groceries, fuel, hardware, building supplies, and sundry other items. The store counted O'Keeffe as one of its customers.

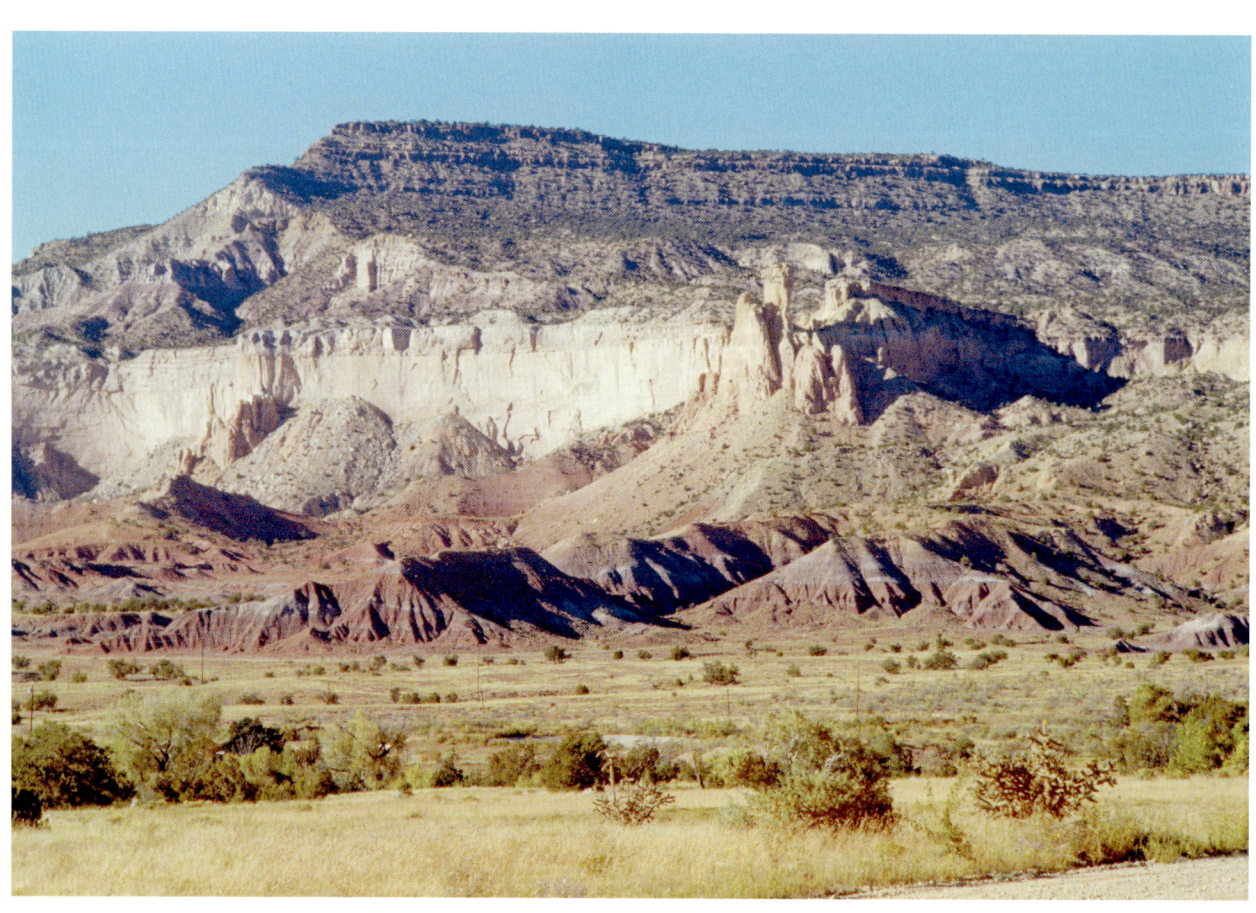

64

Landscape near O'Keeffe's Ghost Ranch house.

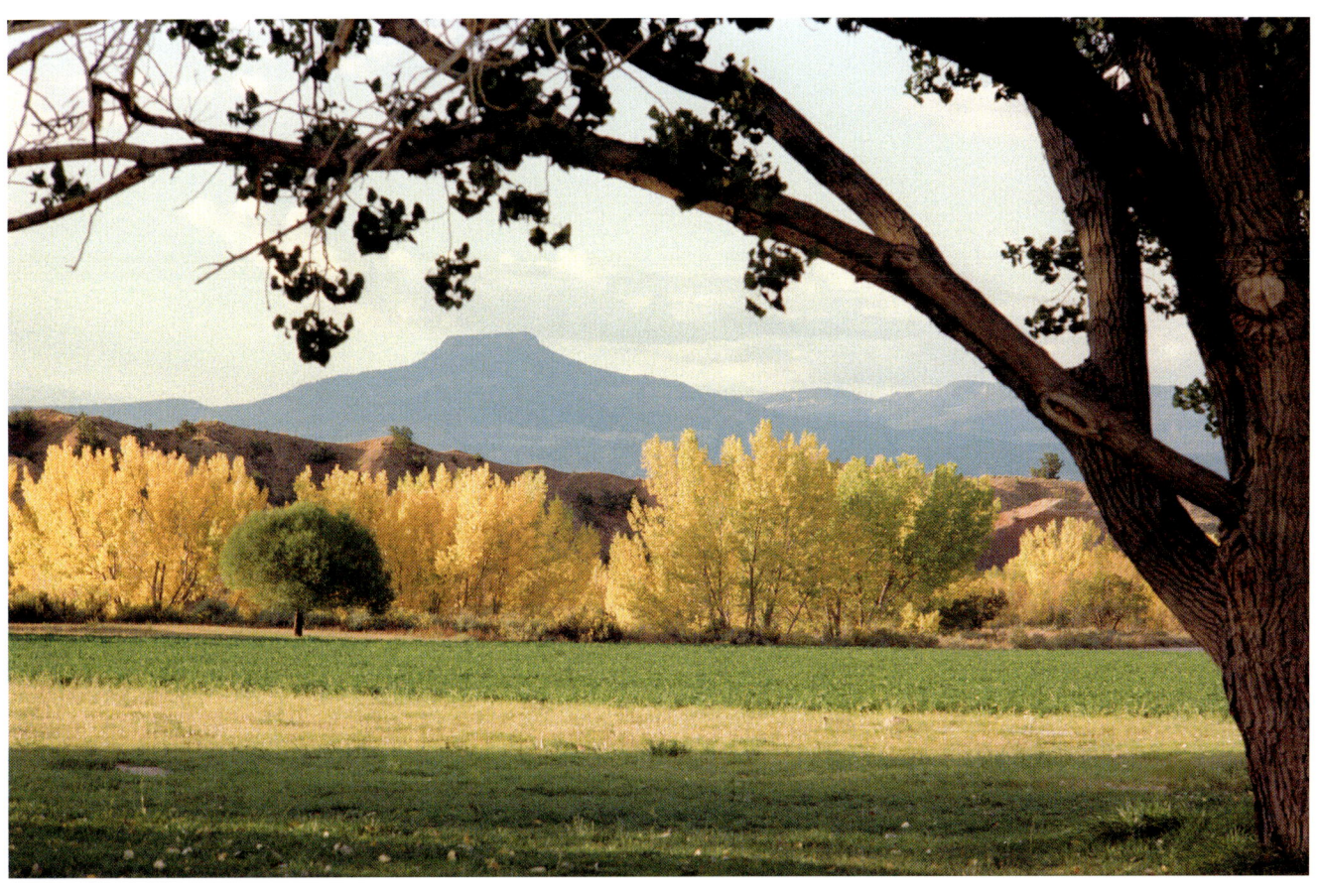

View of the Pedernal from the portion of the Ghost Ranch land that is adjacent to O'Keeffe's property. This portion of the original Ghost Ranch land is owned by the Presbyterian Church and is used as a conference center and retreat. O'Keeffe was able to see pretty much this view of the Pedernal from her Ghost Ranch compound, which is about a mile west of where this photo was taken. The Pedernal was a frequent subject in O'Keeffe's paintings. O'Keeffe's ashes are scattered at its top.

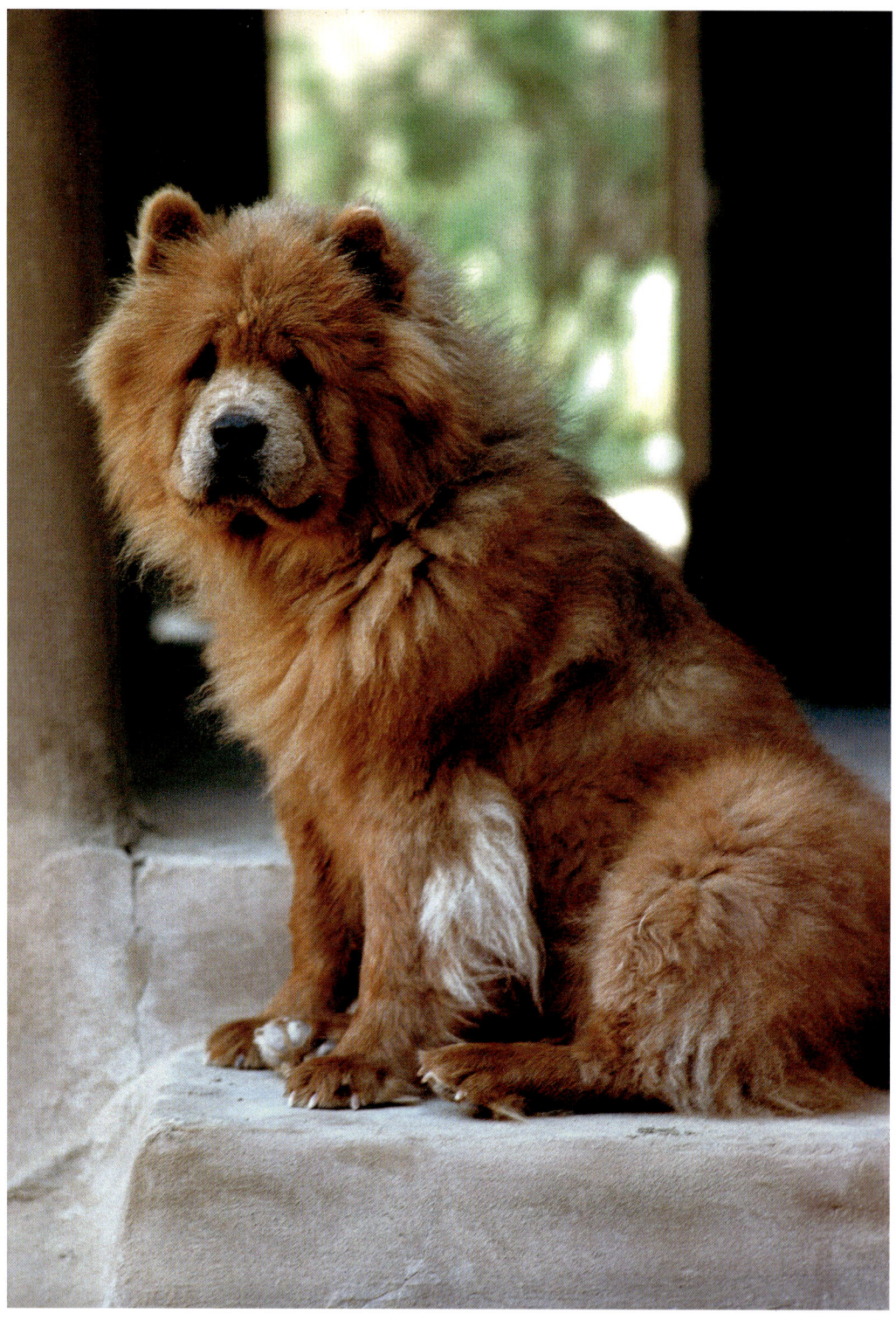

Jingo, a proud and regal animal, was the last of the several Chow dogs O'Keeffe owned during her life. She acquired her first Chows in 1952 and thereafter owned no other breed.

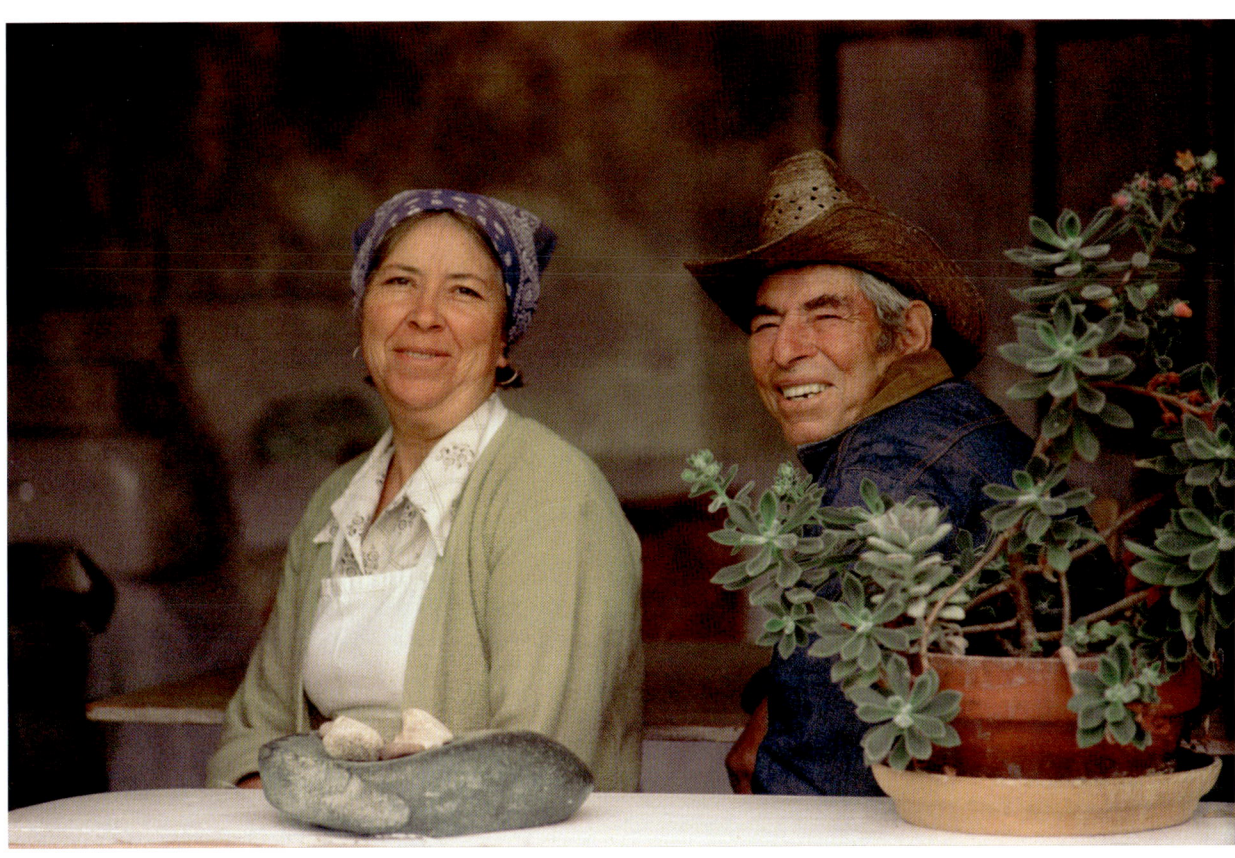

Candelaria Lopez and Estiben Suazo. They are the mother and grandfather
of Agapita Judy Lopez, O'Keeffe's longtime administrative assistant. Candelaria was
employed by O'Keeffe as a cook and housekeeper. She prepared most of O'Keeffe's meals.
Estiben was employed by O'Keeffe to maintain the garden in the compound.

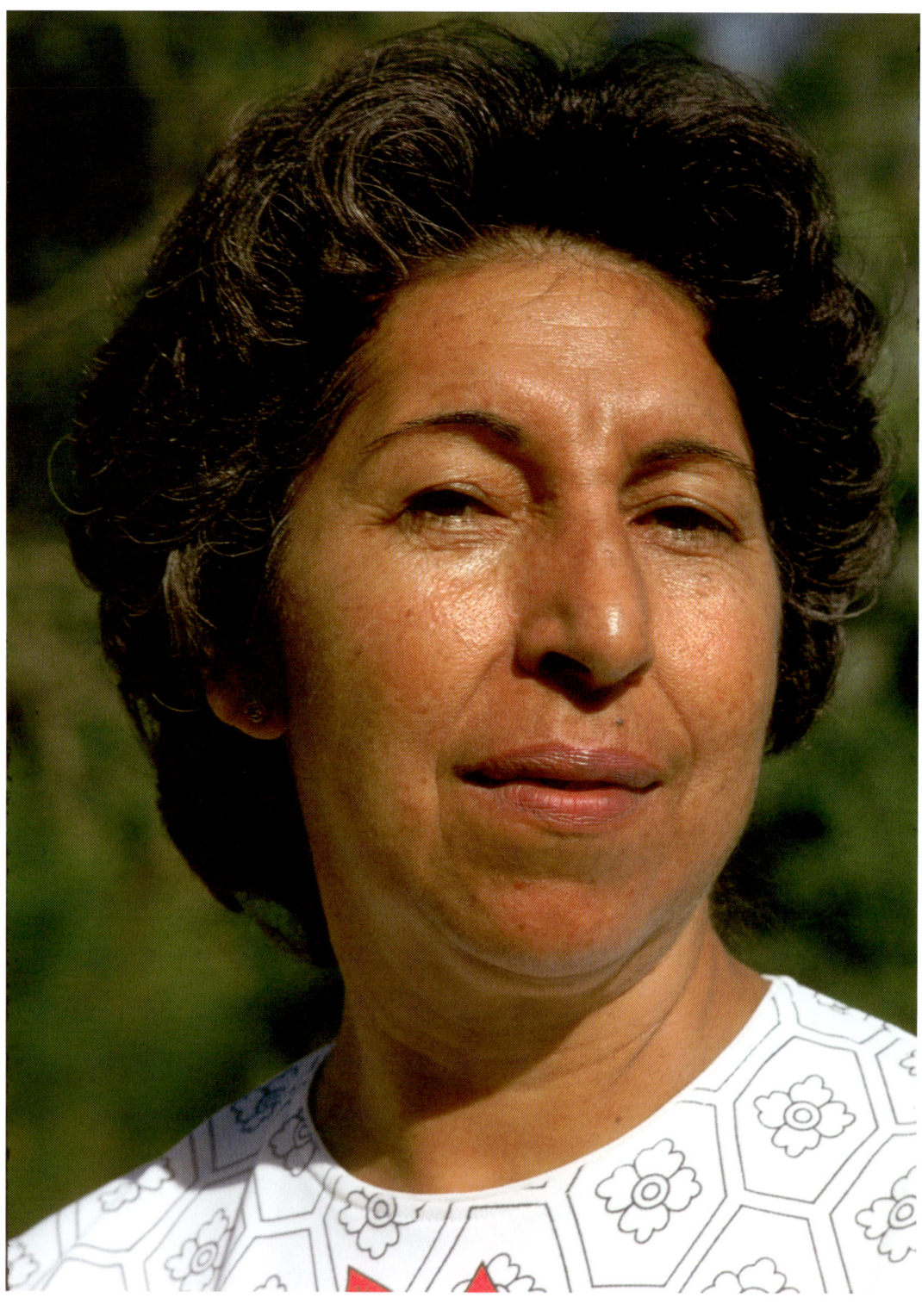

Ida Archuleta, Agapita Judy Lopez's aunt. Ida was employed by O'Keeffe
as a cook and housekeeper. She did much of the baking and pastry making.

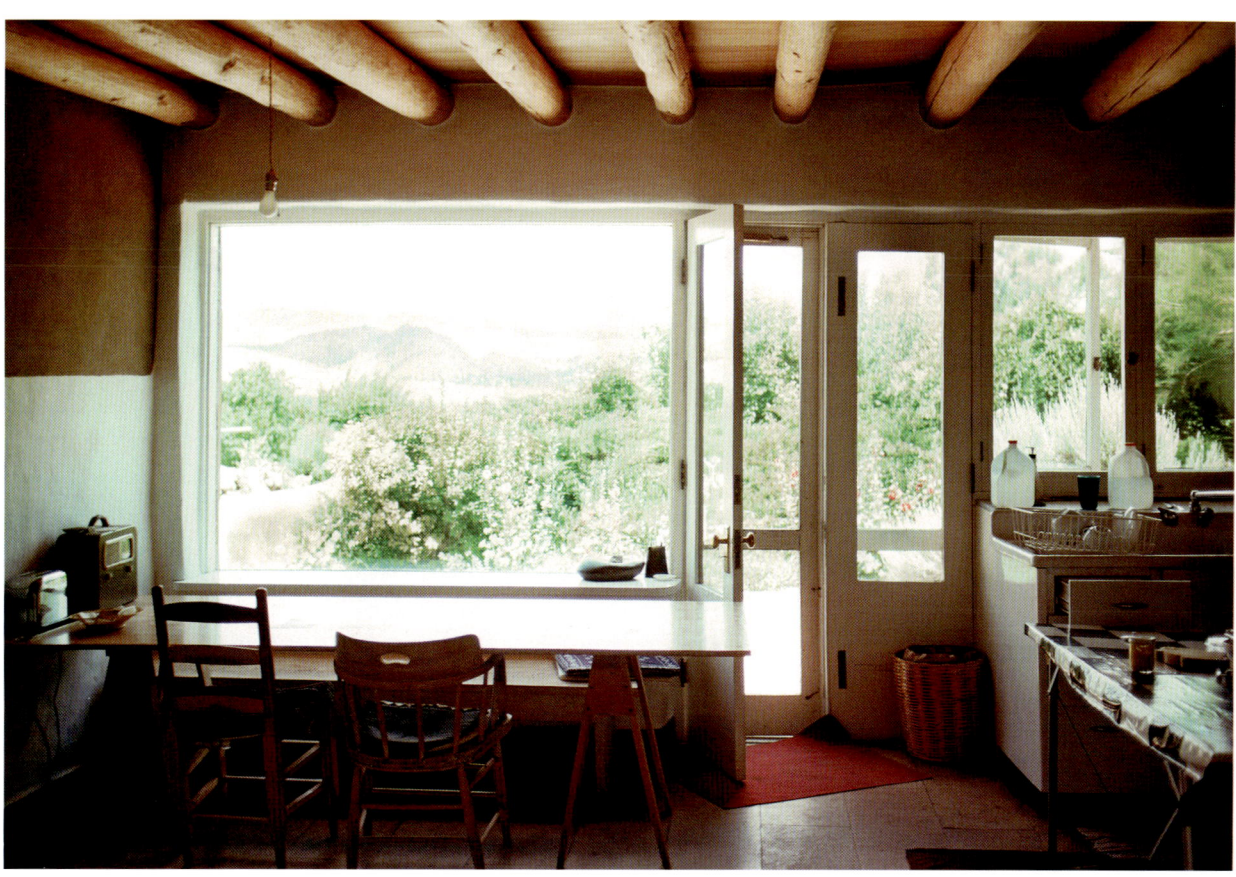

The dining area in O'Keeffe's kitchen at Abiquiú. The appurtenances are simple, in keeping with O'Keeffe's simplicity and lack of ostentation in all of her surroundings, despite having great wealth at this point in her life. The kitchen table, a plank of wood on wooden horses, is another example of her creation of simplicity in her milieu.

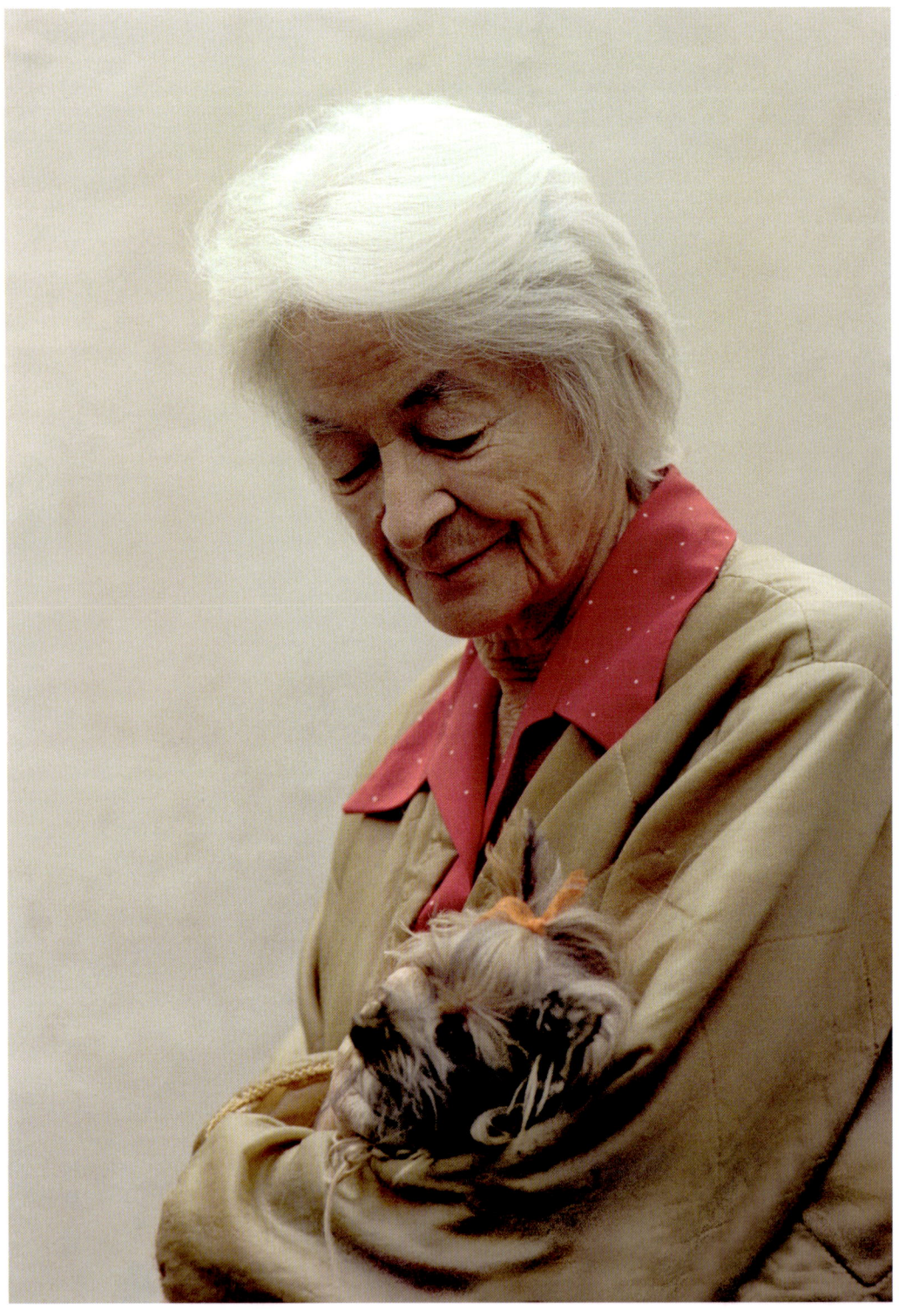

Claudia, O'Keeffe's sister, with her pet dog Suzie. Claudia helped O'Keeffe
with her garden and visited O'Keeffe frequently enough in Abiquiú to have
one of the rooms in the compound designated as "Claudia's room."

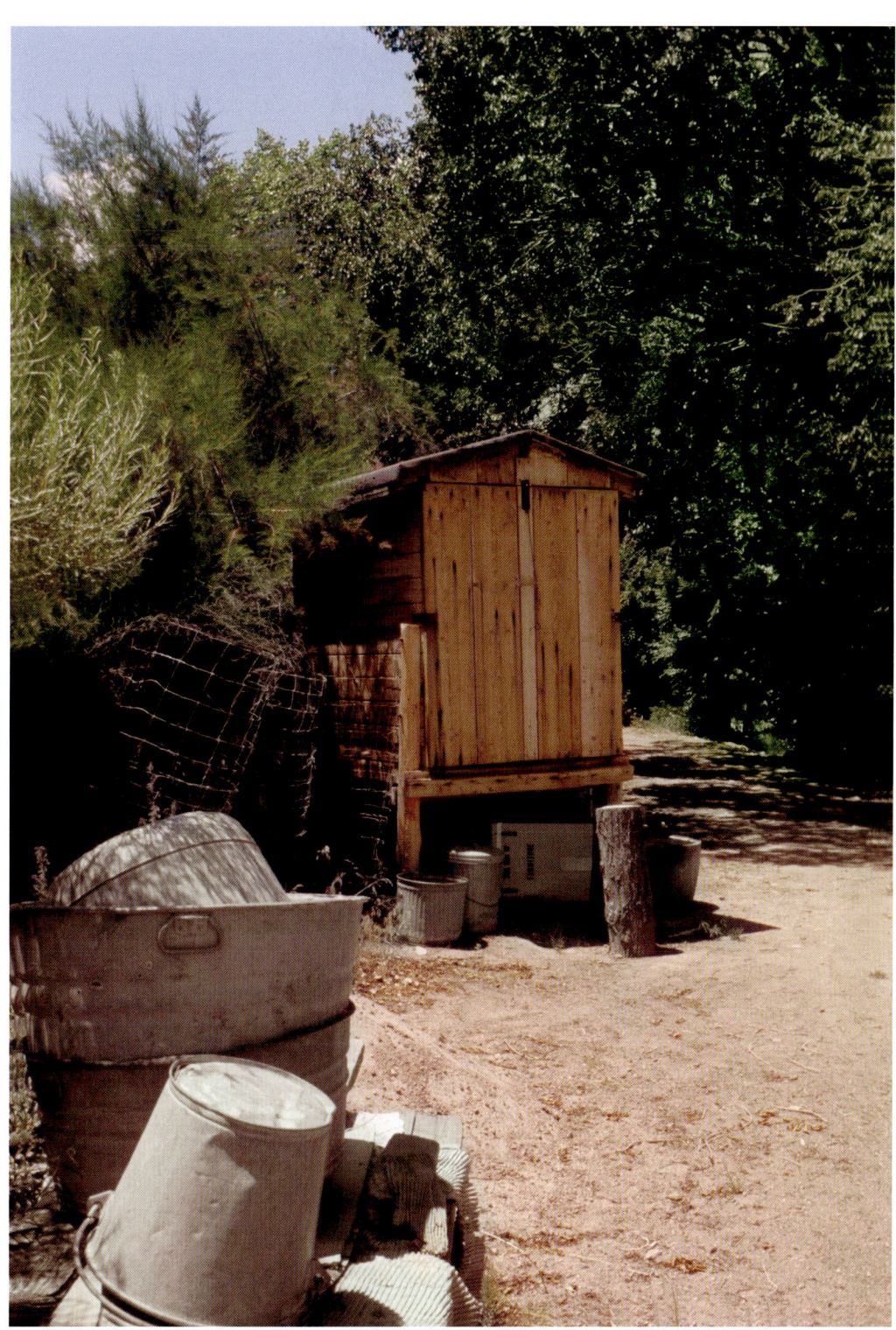

A toolshed adjacent to O'Keeffe's garden at Abiquiú.

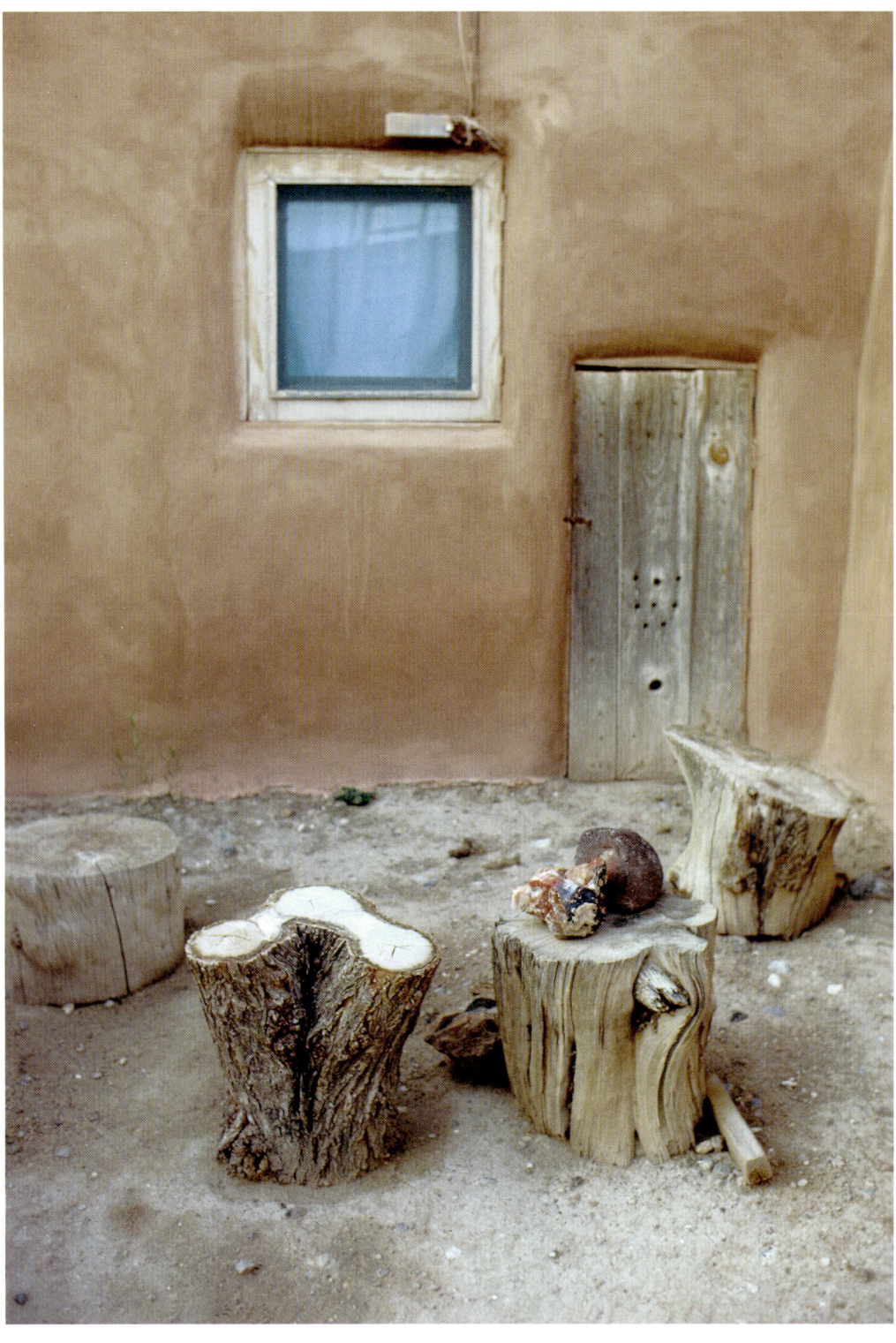

Nothing in the Abiquiú house appeared to be randomly placed. There seemed to be a certain ubiquitous orderliness throughout, but in the service of an aesthetic sensibility. This view of a corner of the patio caught my eye as a particularly pleasing juxtaposition of objects on the ground and in front of the adobe walls of the house.

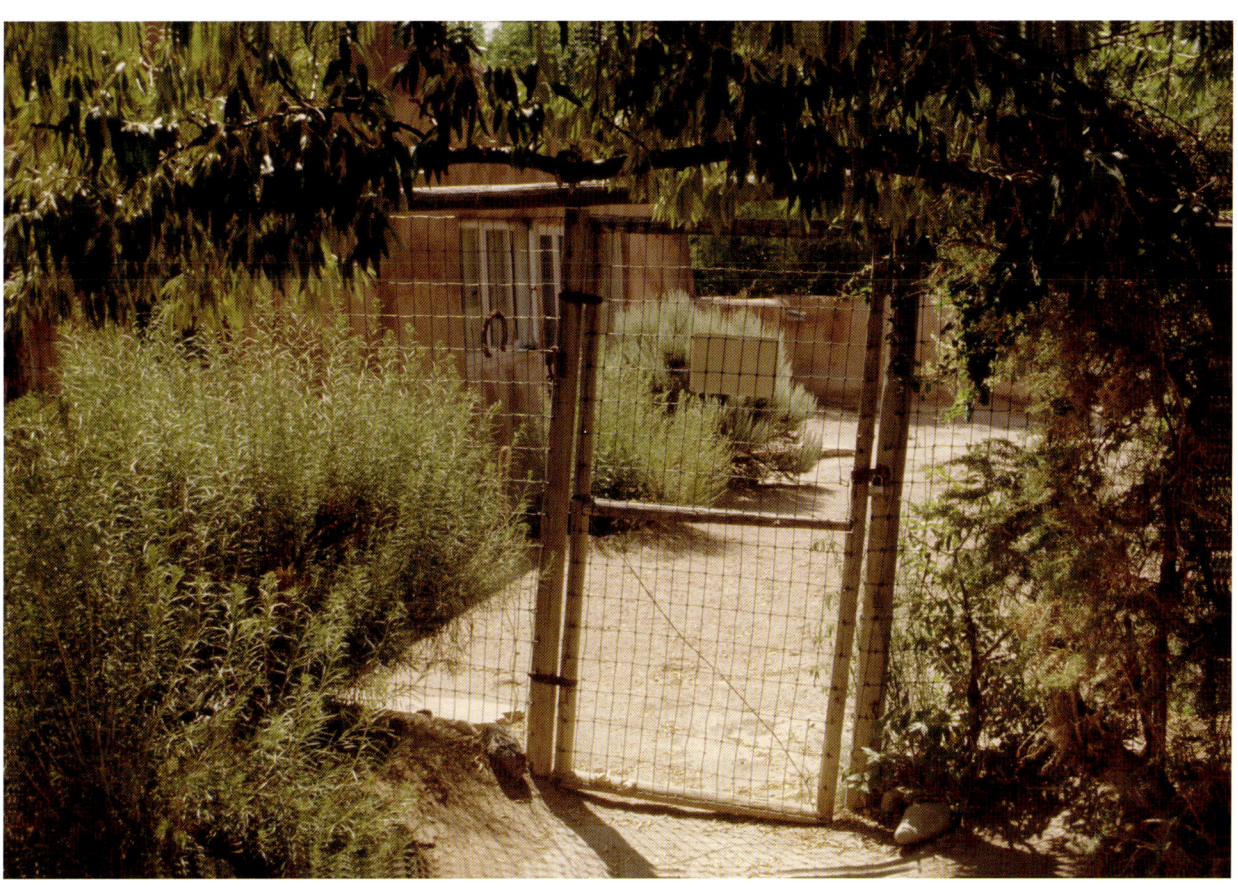

73

This wire gate encloses a small patio-like area, inside
of which you can see the doors to the kitchen on the left.

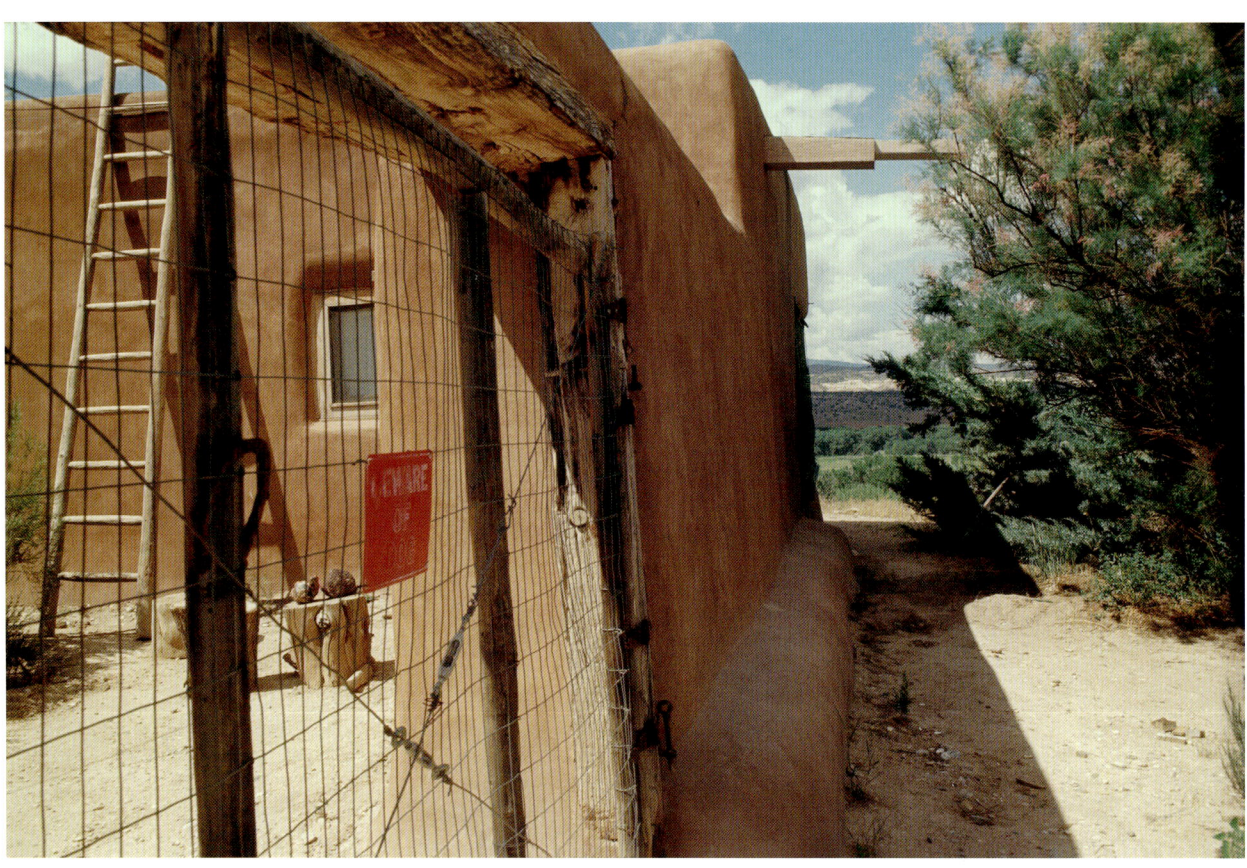

I was fascinated by the color and shapes of the adobe, the hand-hewn logs and tree branches,
the kiva ladders, and the plain wire fencing that made up so much of the visual presence
of O'Keeffe's Abiquiú house. This section of the house particularly drew my attention in that sense.
The view is a pathway along the east wall and encloses O'Keeffe's bedroom and bathroom.

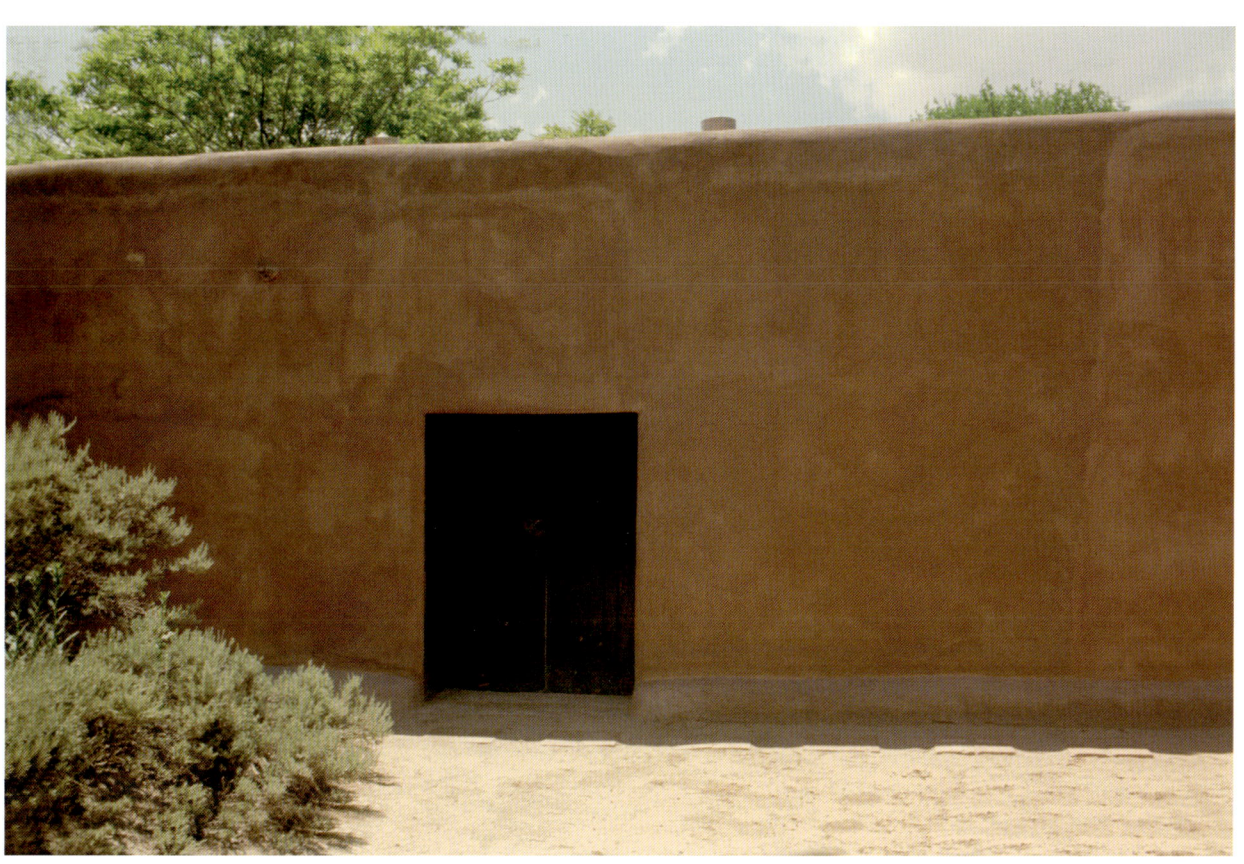

This is the black door in the patio of the Abiquiú house,
which was the subject of several of O'Keeffe's paintings.

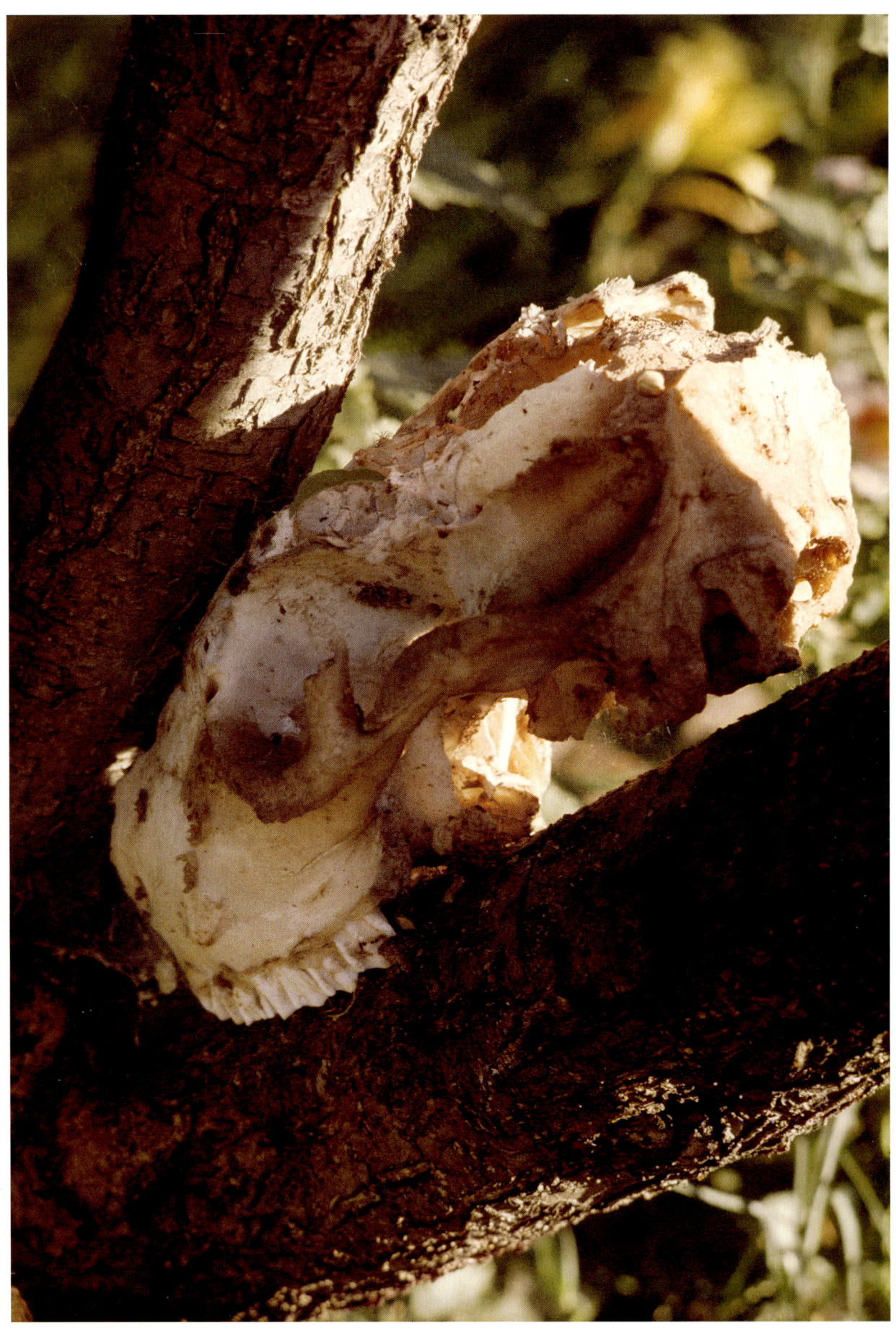

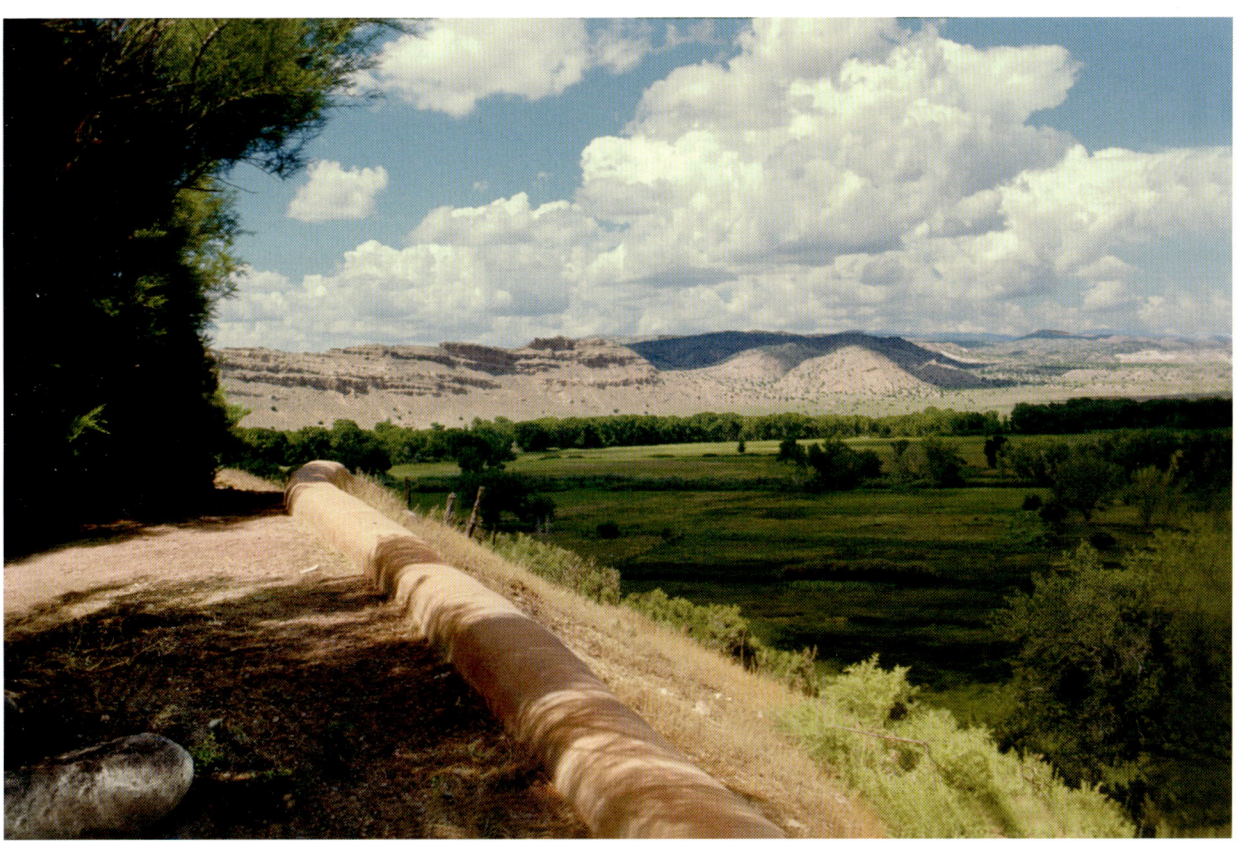

This is a section of the large gravel and clay yard at the front of the main entrance to the Abiquiú house. The low, snakelike adobe structure hugging the ground at the center of the photo is at the northern boundary of the O'Keeffe property. The background is a view of the Chama River Valley.

Opposite page: As I was walking along a path in the garden at Abiquiú I came upon this animal skull, at eye level, wedged in the 'V" shape formed by two tree branches. Although I was already used to seeing skulls, pelvises, and antlers at the Abiquiú and Ghost Ranch houses, this skull deliberately wedged in a tree branch was particularly arresting for me.

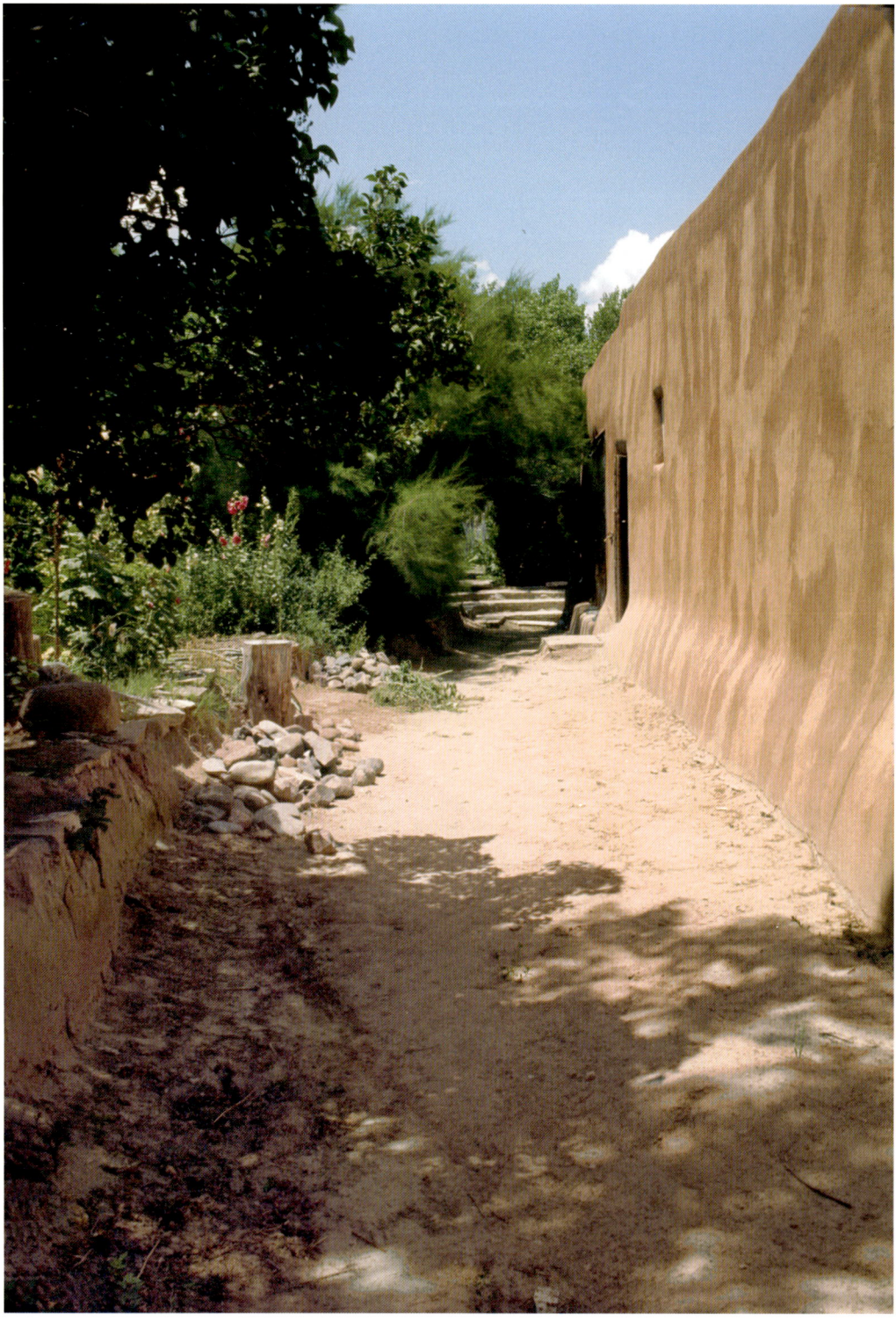

This is a path along a section of the south wall of the Abiquiú house leading to the garden.
Toward the end on the right is the door to a passageway that brings you into the patio.

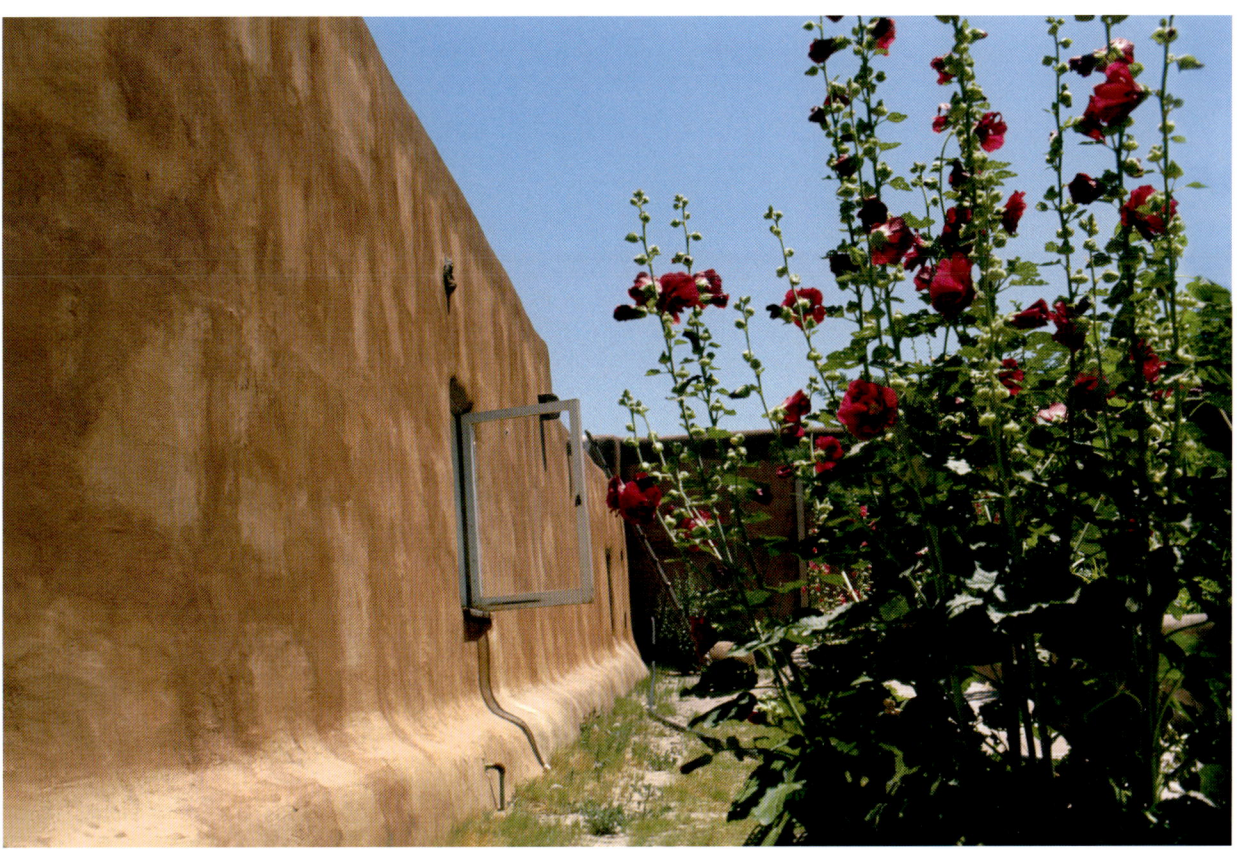

A section of the south wall of the Abiquiú house. This view is facing east.
At the end of the path, on the left, is the opening to the roofless room. Facing you at
the very end is the exterior wall of the sitting room. The garden is on the right.

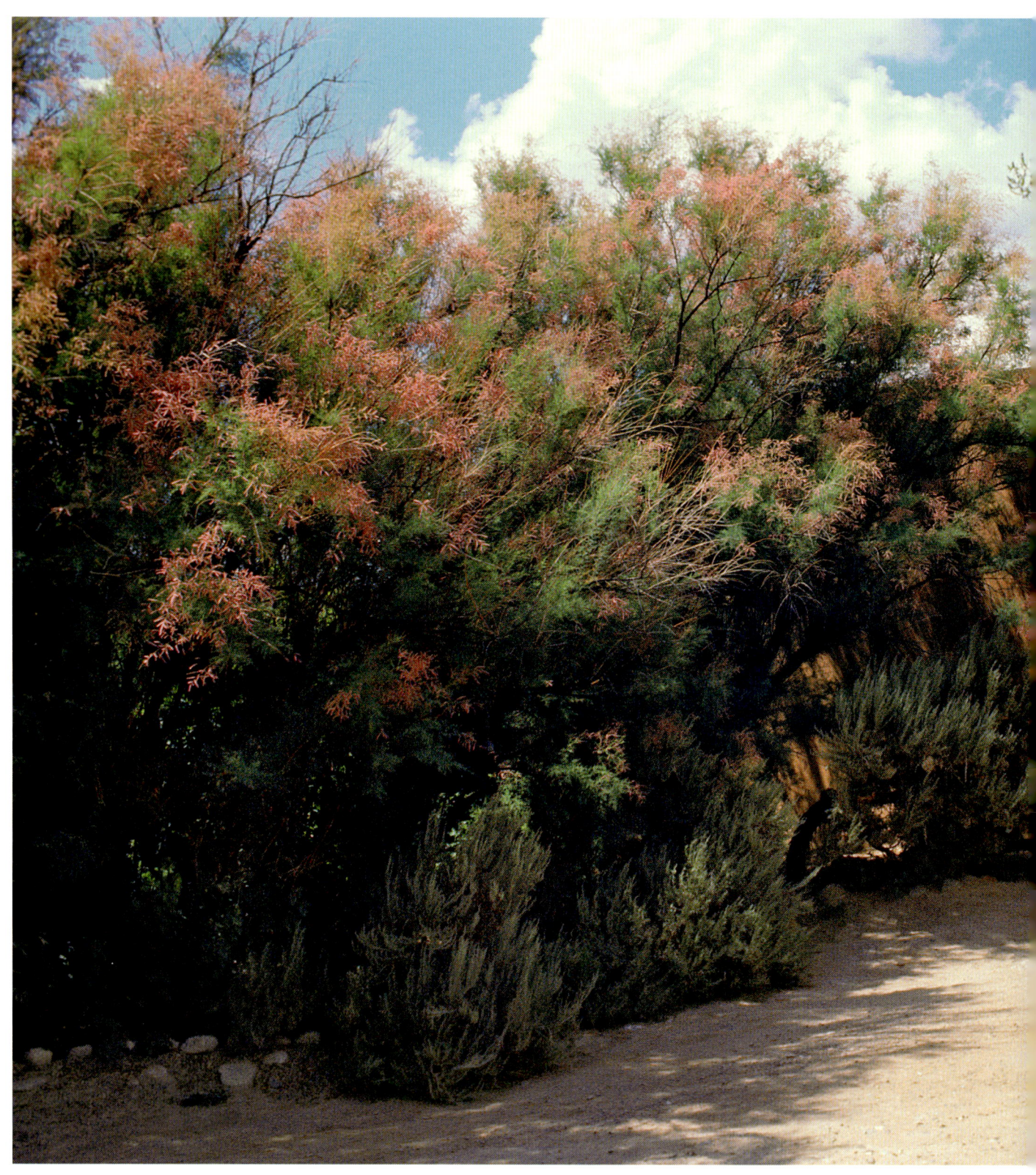

Entrance to O'Keeffe's studio, with a tamarisk tree in bloom on the left.

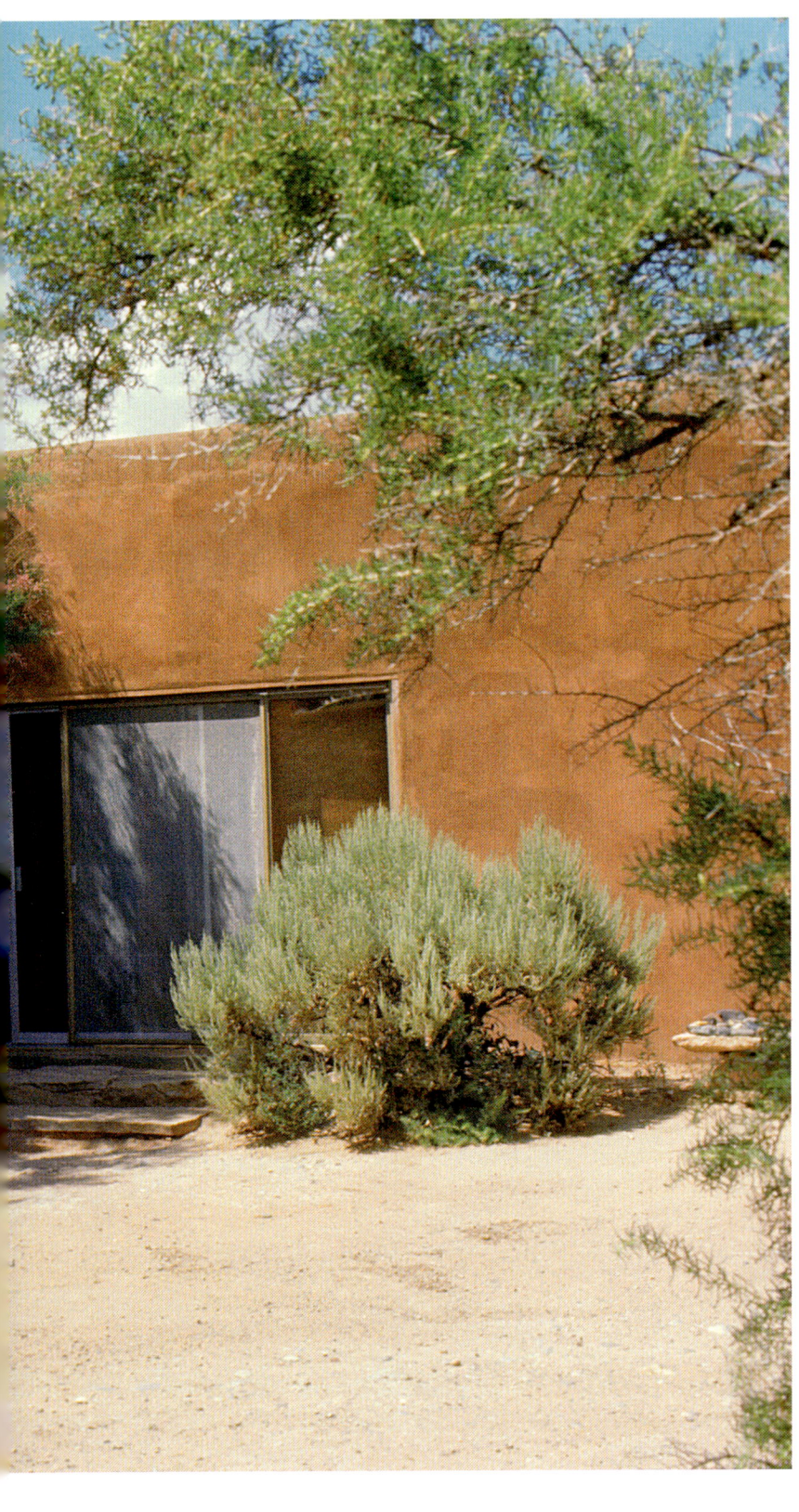

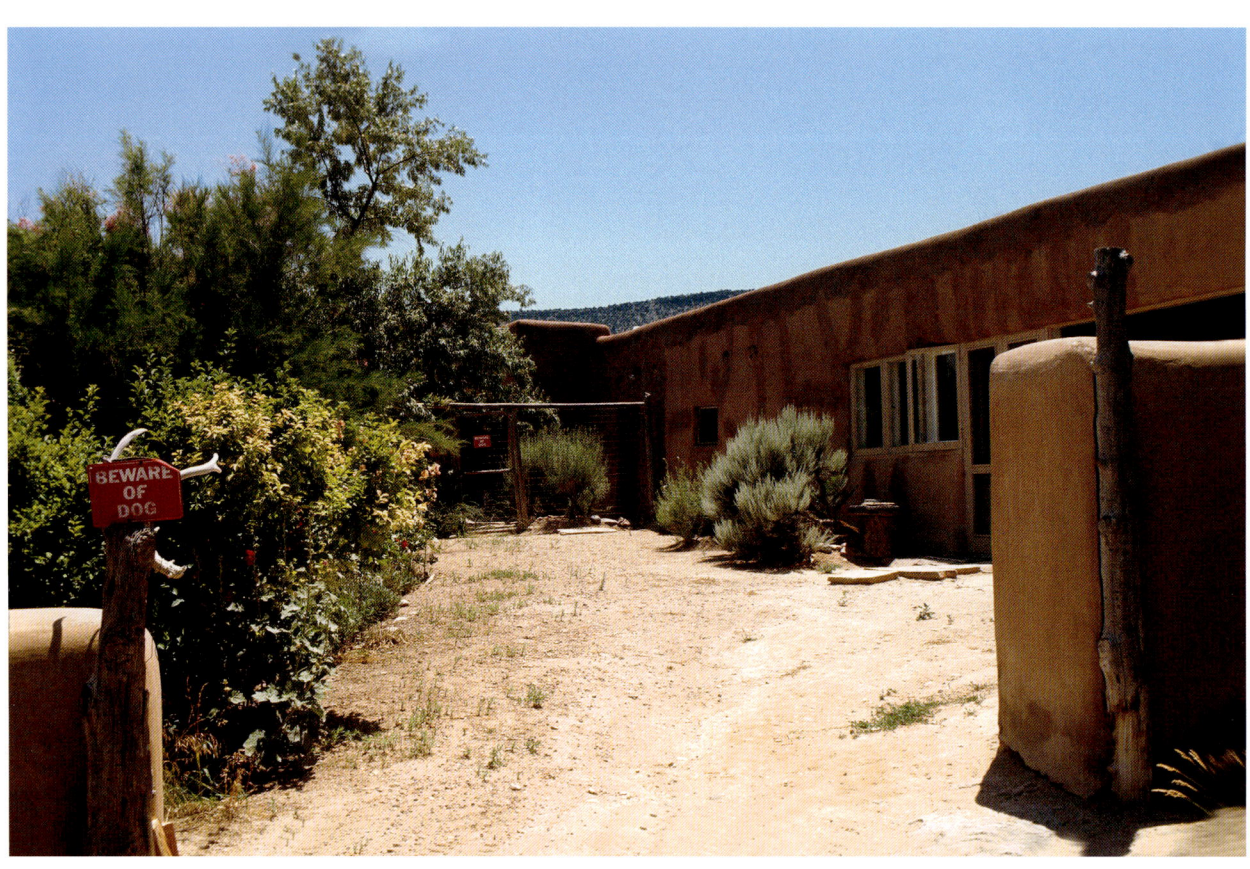

Entranceway to the house from the west wall. The door to the kitchen is on the right.

Opposite page: This photo shows Route I-84 as it comes up from Española and continues north past Abiquiú. The photo was taken from a pathway just outside O'Keeffe's bedroom window at Abiquiú. It is the view of the curve in the road that O'Keeffe mentions in the Viking Press book, *O'Keeffe* (1976), and is essentially a replication of the view she describes seeing and photographing from her bedroom window. In the Viking text she relates that this curving line of the highway as it comes up from Española became the basis for her paintings *The Winter Road*, 1963, and *Road Past the View II*, 1964.

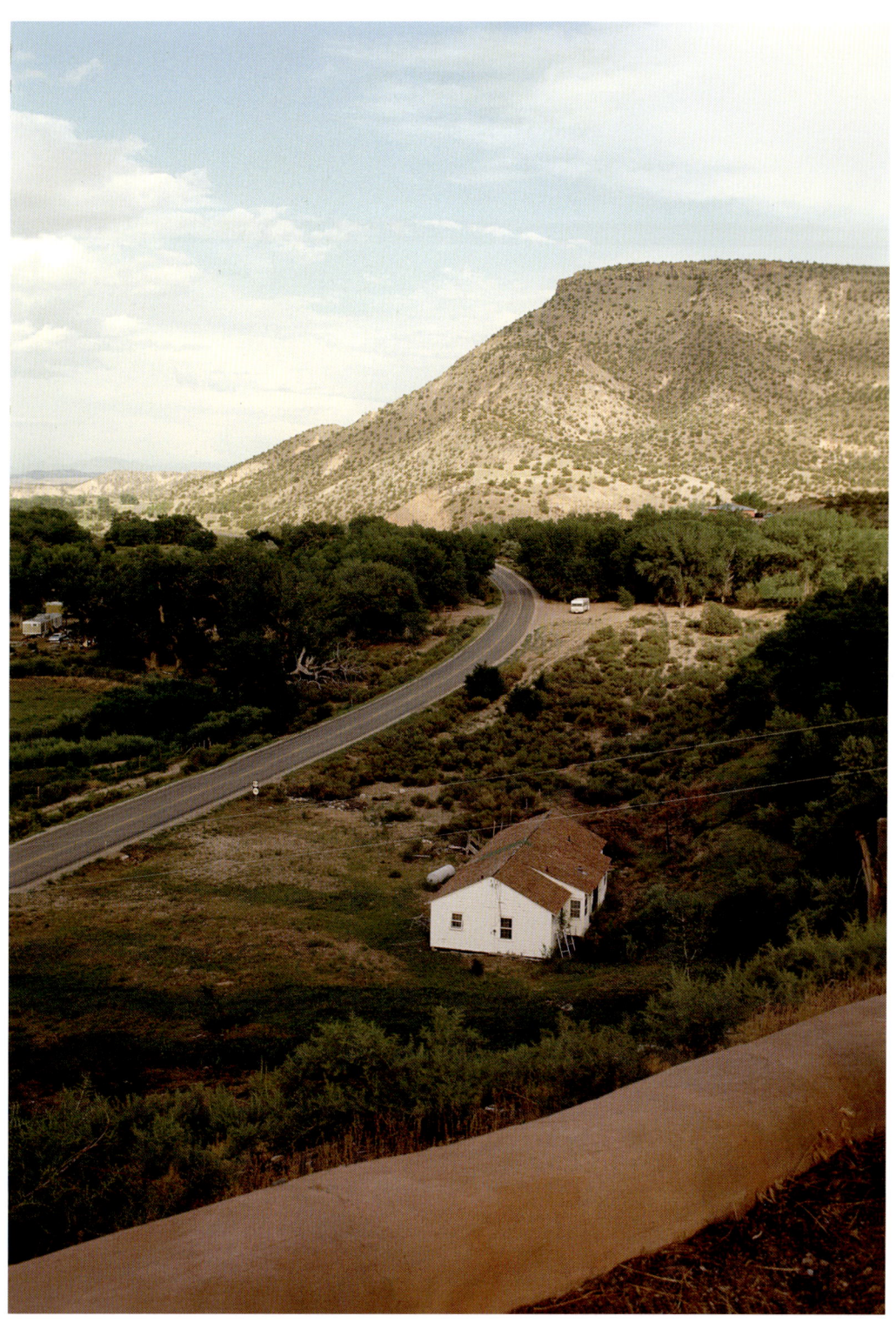

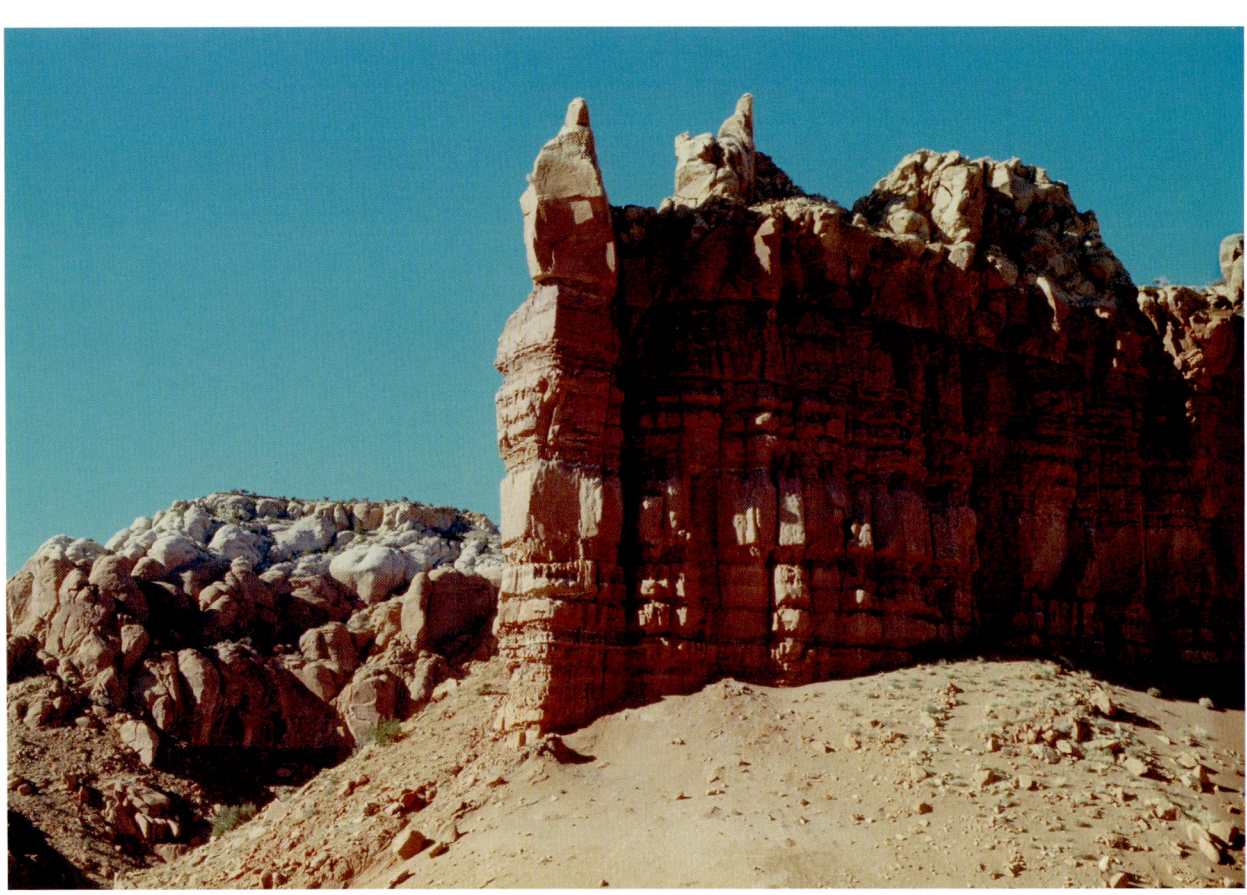

This is a rock formation that looms into view at a curve in the road between Abiquiú and Ghost Ranch. It is an example of the endless varieties of impressive rock formations you can encounter in the northern New Mexico desert in the Abiquiú and Ghost Ranch area.

Opposite page: The sign that stands at the entrance to both Ghost Ranch and the Ghost Ranch Presbyterian Education and Retreat Center. Ghost Ranch is divided between the portion owned by the Presbyterian Church and the portion owned by O'Keeffe, which is now part of the Georgia O'Keeffe Museum. There is an exit road off Route I-84 that extends up a small hill at the top of which is this sign. The road extending beyond this sign brings you to both the O'Keeffe Ghost Ranch complex and the Presbyterian Education and Retreat Center. This view is looking west as you leave Ghost Ranch. The mesa framed by the sign is Orphan Mesa. Route I-84 is actually a few yards away, intersecting this road but obscured by the foreground in the photo.

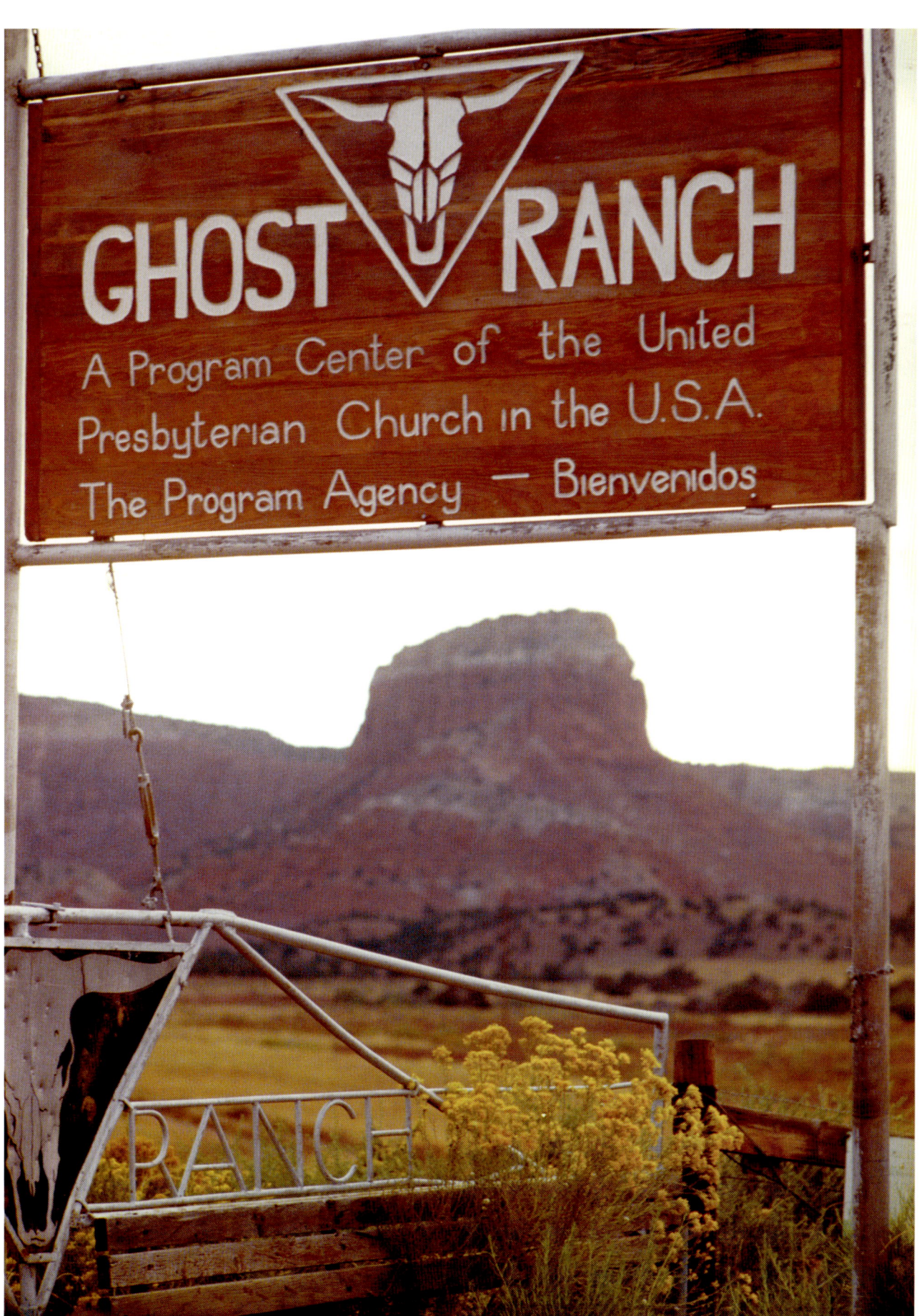

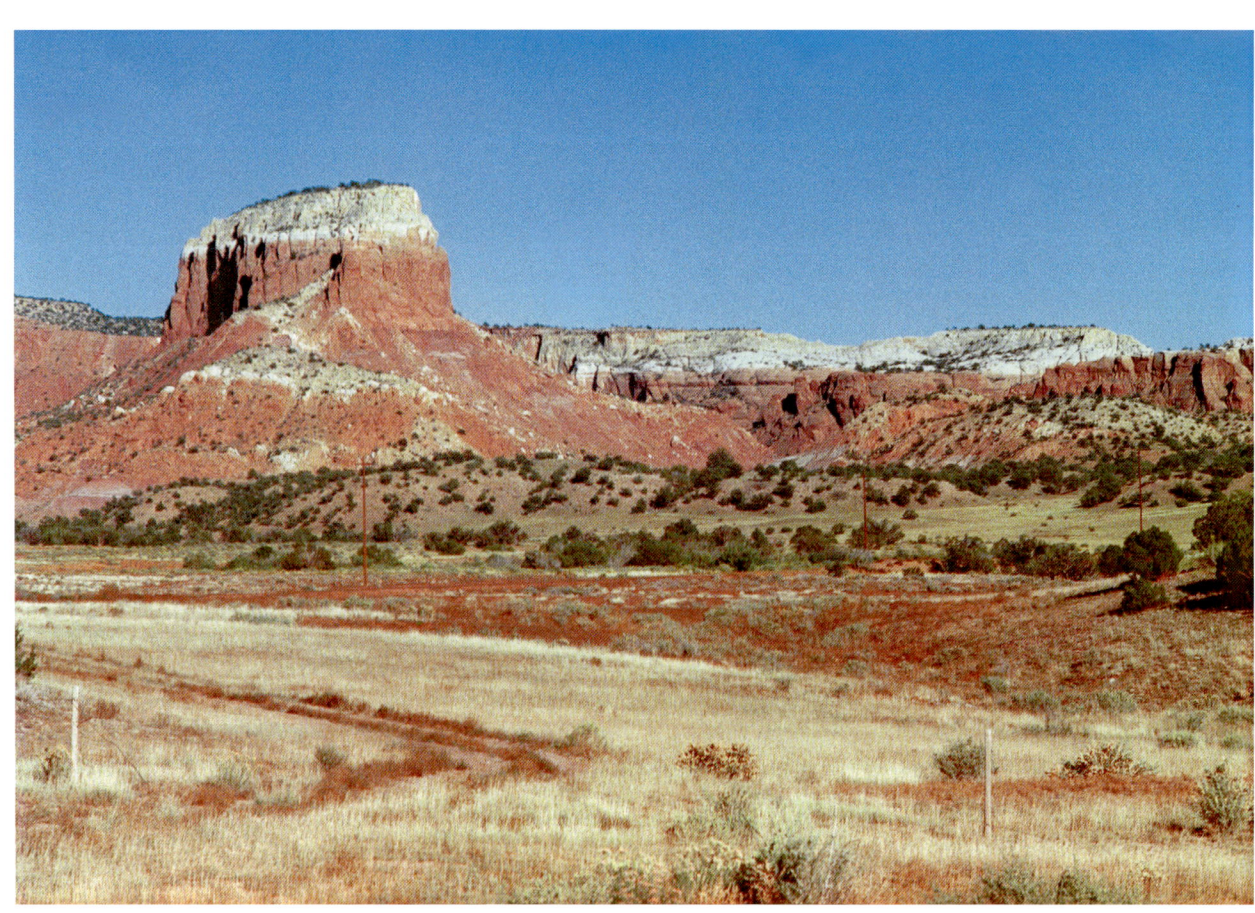

86

Orphan Mesa and the surrounding landscape viewed from Route I-84,
looking west directly opposite the entrance to Ghost Ranch.

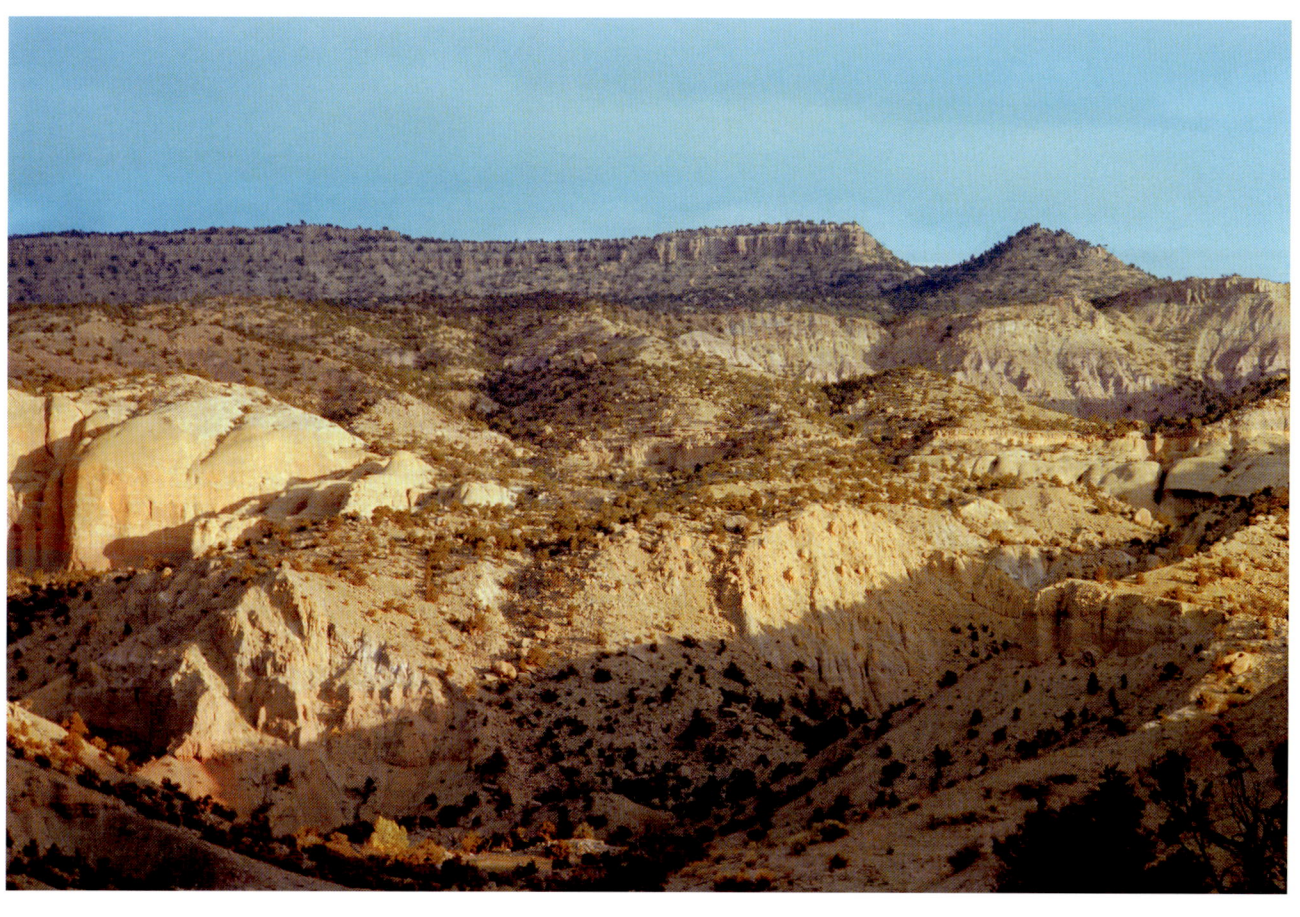

Landscape as seen from Route I-84 between Abiquiú and Ghost Ranch.

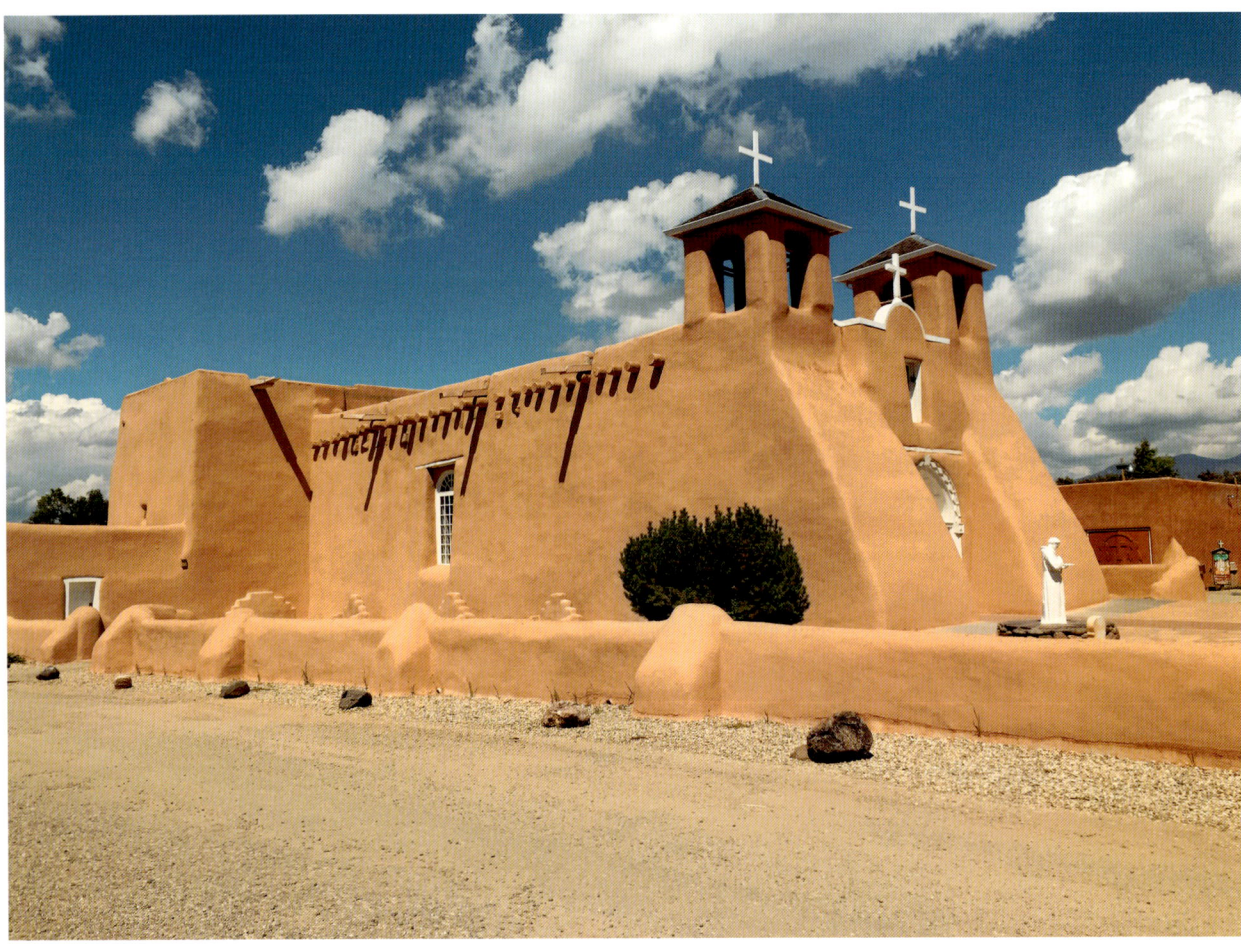

88

Ranchos Church in Taos, New Mexico. O'Keeffe made several paintings of this church,
all as viewed from the rear of the church except for one that is a direct frontal view.

Opposite page: Chama River. As one drives north from Abiquiú toward Ghost Ranch and is on that
part of the road that winds around a mountain shortly after leaving Abiquiú, there are spectacular
views of the Chama River to your left. I took several photos of the Chama River from this general
vantage point. A few years later, on assignment to photograph O'Keeffe's painting *Chama River*,
1937, at the Museum of New Mexico's Museum of Fine Arts, I was astonished to see that O'Keeffe
had painted the river from almost that exact same view some four decades earlier. I should not
have been surprised, however. Whether you're a great painter or basically a tourist taking travel
photos, as I was, it would be hard to resist trying to capture the image of that gorgeous blue river
meandering toward you from the distant mountains.

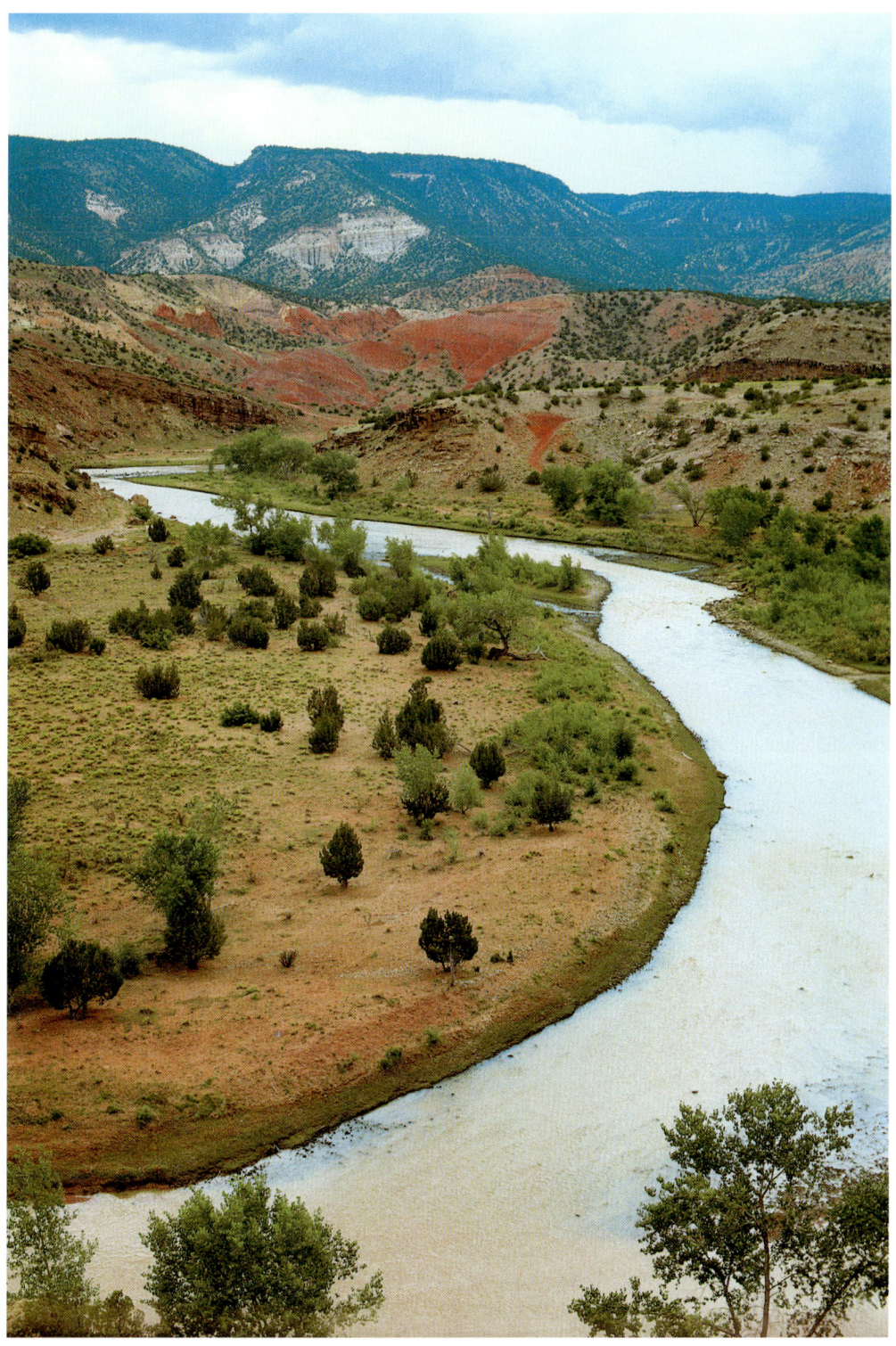

Reflective Essay

MALCOLM VARON

I am one of the least likely of people to have had an association with Georgia O'Keeffe. When I first met O'Keeffe, my interest in the visual arts was minimal. Although I'm a native New Yorker, born and raised in what amounts to a cultural candy store, I had never stepped into an art museum until I was twenty-seven years old, and then only because it was a convenient place to meet a friend.

And yet somehow I became O'Keeffe's photographer of choice when she needed pictures of her paintings. Ultimately, she permitted me to make portraits of her and her environment, which have resulted in the photographs in this book.

Unrelated accidents, serendipities, and chance coalesced into my first meeting with O'Keeffe and the relationship that followed.

WHILE SERVING IN the United States Air Force during the Korean War, I acquired my first camera. I was stationed in Korea during the third year of my four-year tour of duty and bought a 35 mm camera in Japan while en route. I wanted to record my experience of being in a third-world country devastated by war. A year later, upon discharge, I settled into an apartment on the Lower East Side of Manhattan and became friends with some of the young artists and writers who were gravitating there in the early 1960s. Because I was the only one with a camera among the visual artists in my group of friends, I began documenting the paintings of the visual artists, without charge except for the cost of film and processing.

Eventually, at age twenty-seven, I enrolled as a freshman at Hunter College in New York City. I graduated cum laude with a BA in philosophy and was granted a full-tuition fellowship to pursue graduate studies in philosophy at Columbia

University. This endeavor was cut short in 1966 by a family member's illness, which obliged me to leave graduate school and become a caretaker.

In order to have flexible hours and yet earn a living, I started doing freelance photography, making color slides of paintings. After much reading in photography and color theory and lots of practice, I acquired enough skill to be hired by the Museum of Modern Art and the Metropolitan Museum of Art to make documentary slides of paintings. This soon segued into making large-format transparencies of paintings for those museums and others, for reproduction in museum catalogues and coffee-table art books.

By 1969 my photography credits for painting reproductions caught the attention of Doris Bry, who was O'Keeffe's manager, friend, and general administrator. She contacted me and asked me to come to her apartment to photograph an O'Keeffe painting. I initially treated the request as any other—a person had a painting they wanted photographed. It was common for people whom I didn't know to contact me for that purpose. I had never seen or photographed an O'Keeffe painting, nor did I know who O'Keeffe was, so I asked my assistant to do some research before I met Bry. I later realized she was testing me to see if I could accurately photograph O'Keeffe's work.

Bry lived in a large apartment across from the Whitney Museum of American Art, in what appeared to be a building that was once an ornate mansion with lots of marble and a long staircase leading to the second-floor rooms that she occupied. As befit such a stately environment, Bry herself was a very tall and elegant woman, with striking white hair. Bry ushered me into her apartment, and in a very businesslike manner set the painting to be photographed in front of me. I proceeded to set up my lights and camera, shot the painting, and left.

I don't remember which painting it was. In fact, in the roughly fifteen years of my association with O'Keeffe, I never took notes about any interaction between us. It was a business connection that I never had any intention to write about, but I am doing so now to put my photographs in this book in context.

A few days after the shoot, I presented Bry with my color-corrected 8 × 10 transparency. She thought it was one of the most accurate renditions of an O'Keeffe painting that she had thus far been able to obtain, and she immediately hired me to come to New Mexico with her to photograph a recent painting by O'Keeffe.

We flew to New Mexico a week later, arriving at the Albuquerque airport, where we were picked up by one of O'Keeffe's staff and driven to Ghost

Ranch, about 135 miles northwest of Albuquerque. It was a rainy, dreary night, which I discovered during my subsequent visits was unusual weather for that area. Upon arrival at Ghost Ranch I was shown the painting to be photographed. It was large, 8 × 24 feet, and hanging in the back of a two-car garage on the Ghost Ranch complex. I immediately set up my lights and camera and photographed it, taking advantage of the fact that it was night-time, which therefore allowed me to easily control the quality of my light. That particular painting I remember well. It was *Sky Above Clouds IV*, 1965. The photograph I took on that cold night was used as the wraparound cover of the Whitney Museum of American Art catalogue for the 1970 O'Keeffe Retrospective exhibition.

I stayed overnight at Ghost Ranch, sleeping on a cot in an adobe room with a mud floor, and left for the airport the next morning to fly back to New York. I had never been to the Southwest before except for my time on a US Air Base in El Paso, and this experience was eerily dreamlike to me as a city dweller.

For the next few years I shot O'Keeffe paintings in New York City and its environs and also occasionally in Abiquiú, O'Keeffe's other New Mexico home, about fifteen miles south of Ghost Ranch. It was during this period, in 1973 or 1974, that I met Juan Hamilton, who at the time was working as a general assistant to O'Keeffe. O'Keeffe had asked me to photograph some paintings in a New York City warehouse, and she sent Juan to make the appropriate arrangements and oversee the photography. My assignment was to create the photographs of O'Keeffe's paintings for publication in the first coffee-table art book devoted entirely to her art. She was to be the author, writing an autobiographical text relating to the paintings. Viking Press was the publisher.

Approximately three years later, as O'Keeffe was approaching her ninetieth birthday, she asked me to come out to Abiquiú to shoot more of the paintings that she still owned and which were located in the Abiquiú house. As a result I spent a good part of the late summer and early autumn of 1977 photographing those paintings. O'Keeffe graciously housed me and my assistant in guest rooms in the Abiquiú compound. Given my nonstop work schedule in New York City, working in O'Keeffe's environment was like a mini-vacation with a little work thrown in as an interesting activity to break up the day. The days were all sunny, the sky an incredibly clear, saturated blue with no haze, and the weather warm. We started work at a reasonable hour, had a leisurely lunch break, and stopped work at around five, while there were still hours of daylight left to take walks and explore the village of Abiquiú or drive to the famous Ojo Caliente Hot Springs a short distance to the east.

It was during this stay that a journalist from *Art News*, Mary Lynn Kotz, came to Abiquiú to interview O'Keeffe for a special edition of the magazine that was to feature an article commemorating O'Keeffe's ninetieth birthday. Kotz wanted some recent photographs of O'Keeffe to include in the article. I offered to make the photographs on a speculative basis, stipulating that I would charge a fee only if the photographs were published. Kotz accepted my offer, and O'Keeffe agreed to be photographed. I spent the next couple of days photographing O'Keeffe and Juan in and around the Abiquiú house and at Ghost Ranch. Several of those photographs were published in the December 1977 issue of *Art News*. And now most of them, taken over those two days, appear in this book for the first time.

DURING THE TIME I spent in the Abiquiú compound in the summer of 1977, my assistant and I often had lunch with O'Keeffe and Juan. Lunch conversation with O'Keeffe did not include any conversation about art. I would never have presumed to discuss anything in that area with O'Keeffe. We did, however, have lively discussions about nutrition. O'Keeffe was very serious about the necessity of a healthy lifestyle, as was I, and proper nutrition was a big part of that. Vegetables were organically grown in O'Keeffe's garden, and meat was imported from a reputable supplier. The meals were cooked by an Abiquiú resident, Candelaria, the mother of Agapita Judy Lopez, who was an invaluable administrative assistant to O'Keeffe.

The daily workings of the house and grounds, and the people necessary to their functioning, were overseen by Juan. Although a native Texan, he was fluent in Spanish, having spent his childhood in Costa Rica, where his father had relocated to work with the Presbyterian Church.

It was apparent to me that Juan held a very important position in O'Keeffe's personal life as well as in her business life. In particular, it appeared that he was not only O'Keeffe's trusted friend but that he also had an active part in helping her sell her paintings. He also functioned as a kind of chief of staff, sorting out who O'Keeffe was willing to give access to and who she was not. It was clear that despite a sixty-year age difference between them, there was a profound depth to their friendship. Juan was the only person I observed who could make O'Keeffe laugh. When they were together they appeared to me as equal human beings sharing a deep, loving, and playful interaction. It seemed that their obvious respect and admiration for each other both as people and as artists created a bond that transcended the disparity in their ages.

AS ONE OF the few people still alive who actually knew O'Keeffe, I want to conclude with some observations and experiences that affected the photographs I took while in her orbit.

O'Keeffe's Abiquiú house was built around a courtyard, and there were various passageways in the sprawling compound to get from one set of rooms to another. In order to get to my makeshift photo studio, I had to walk through a passageway that led to a sitting room, beyond which was my studio. The sitting room was built of adobe, as was most of the house. The floor was hardened mud, and for sitting there was a long bench, also made of adobe. As I was walking through these passages one day, upon entering the sitting room I heard the sound of Wanda Landowska's recording of Bach's *Well-Tempered Clavier* wafting through the air and emanating as though from hidden speakers in the ceiling. The juxtaposition of one of the musical high points of Western culture in the embrace of this ancient adobe tradition was startling.

Most photographs of O'Keeffe in her later years show her with very wrinkled skin, and my photographs in color accentuate its leathery, weather-beaten appearance. But in fact her skin was soft and silky. I discovered this one evening while at dinner with O'Keeffe and Juan after the opening of the 1983 exhibition of Alfred Stieglitz photographs at the National Gallery of Art in Washington, DC. I arrived at the restaurant where we were to meet, and I gave O'Keeffe a little friendly peck of a kiss on her cheek in greeting. To my great astonishment my lips came into contact with a skin that was soft and pliant. This experience was an addendum to my personal experience of O'Keeffe, who radiated a youthfulness that belied her age or appearance.

My photographs of O'Keeffe walking in fields at Ghost Ranch show her with a cane. This seemed a little strange to me, since I had never seen her use a cane around the house. When I asked her about the cane, pointing out her apparent ability to walk very well without it, her reply was that she took the cane with her on walks outside to shoo away the rattlesnakes that might cross her path!

In my photographs of O'Keeffe alone, I tried to capture the intensity of her personality and the piercing, intelligent person you felt could see into you, through you, and beyond you. In my photographs of O'Keeffe and Juan together, I tried to capture the strong and tender connection that existed between them, and also Juan's fiercely protective and caring attitude toward O'Keeffe.

Photographs tell stories, those intended by the photographer and those read into them by the viewer. They create moods, they excite emotions, and they speak to an aesthetic sensibility. I hope my photographs do all those things and provide an expanded sense of O'Keeffe as the extraordinary person I found her to be.

MALCOLM VARON
NEW YORK CITY
FEBRUARY 17, 2020

96

ISBN 978-0-8263-6200-1 (cloth)

Library of Congress Control Number: 2020933603

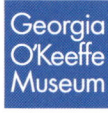

This book was made possible in part by generous contributions from
the Georgia O'Keeffe Museum, the Martin Z. Margulies Foundation, and Willa Bandler.

Front and back cover photographs courtesy of Malcolm Varon
Designed by Felicia Cedillos
Composed in Dante MT Std 12/18